THE TRANSFORMED FAMILY

Revelations That Will Help Your Family Reach Its Destiny

BY

PAUL M. GOULET

The Transformed Family
ISBN: 978-0-615-22098-7
© 2008 by the International Church of Las Vegas
8100 Westcliff Drive
Las Vegas, NV 89145
www.ICLV.com

Cover Design by Renee Fabiano
Edited by Stefan Konstantopoulos

Published by:
The International Church of Las Vegas
8100 Westcliff Drive
Las Vegas, NV 89145
USA

Printed by www.devtechprinters.com

DEDICATION

I dedicate this book to the five most important women in my life:

MY MOM: You are an incredible woman of faith at 87.

MY WIFE: You have taught me more about being a parent than any book.

MY SISTER: You helped raise me and prayed me into the faith.

MY DAUGHTER ISABELLE: You are the eldest of our children and a bright light. We've learned a lot from you and you will always be my sunshine. I love you.

MY DAUGHTER CHRISTINE: Though you are the middle child, you have done an incredible job leading others from the middle of the pack. You inspire me. I love you.

CONTENTS

ACKNOWLEDGEMENTS

The list of friends, family members, teachers, mentors, staff and colleagues who contributed directly and indirectly to *The Transformed Family* would probably be longer than the book itself. I do, however, want to single-out two people for special recognition:

First, I would like to convey heartfelt gratitude to my assistant Norma Urrabazo. Your hard work, loyalty, reliability and administrative gifts are truly an enormous blessing to our church and to me. Your faithful and efficient service frees me to pursue many goals and callings. One of which was the writing of this book.

I also want to express sincere appreciation to Michelle Kennedy, for using your careful and capable eyes to proofread, critique, amend and correct the rough pages of the written words of this book. The fact that you can interpret my handwriting is still a wonder. You are loved and appreciated.

FOREWORD BY DR. RICHARD DOBBINS

From the moment I saw the influence Pastor Paul Goulet had on his graduate peers in my seminary classroom, I knew he was destined to be a great leader in the church. Through the years I have seen God use him to impact the lives of thousands of people. Yet, his most impressive accomplishment is seen in his pursuit of God's best for his personal life, his marriage and his family. Maintaining those priorities is largely responsible for the transparent authenticity which multiplies his impact on others.

From humble beginnings in their church in Las Vegas, Pastors Paul and Denise Goulet have built one of the world's great missionary churches. In spite of his energy-demanding schedule of missionary evangelism, Pastor Paul has refused to neglect his personal priorities. Learning from the tragic failures of other great ministries, Pastor Paul, in this book, dispenses invaluable, practical lessons for keeping marriages and families together, in a world where they are falling apart.

This is not only the kind of book you will want to read again, but you will also want to recommend it to others.

FOREWORD BY MIKE GOTTFRIED

During my twenty-one years working as a coach, I observed the effects of godly parents who failed to influence their sons and daughters. In football, every winning team has a playbook. This is a playbook for the Christ-centered family.

The Transformed Family contains biblically-based strategies and practical insights that will help you transform your family. Pastor Paul reveals God's plan for the family and His heart for each family member. Whether you are a father, mother, grandparent or poised to start a family one day, *The Transformed Family* will be a tremendous resource for you.

THE JOURNEY TO OUR DESTINY

The title of this introduction speaks so loudly about the direction of this book and my personal life philosophy: *"Children are a heritage from the Lord; the fruit of the womb is a reward."* (Psalm 127:3) I believe that God is very much a part of my life and family. For 28 years my wife and I have been on an amazing journey that is preparing us for our ultimate destiny and those of our children. In fact, this journey is the foundation and breath that will one day be recognized as our legacy. This book is not a child-rearing manual; it is a construction journal (or road map) designed to launch you and your family on your journey of destiny and purpose.

I've been very troubled by the recent rash of moral failures and marital collapses of high-profile pastors and ministers. These individuals, with national exposure, were surrounded by a great cloud of witnesses. So many people have been damaged and disillusioned by these lapses in judgment, morals or convictions. I don't think it is important to create a list of infamy to press this point into our souls. I think that you probably know who I am referring to; nevertheless, we've all felt the sting of these stories.

Although I too have been disappointed, I have to admit that I have not been completely surprised. Throughout the past 25 years of ministry, I have had the privilege of being with the best and brightest of evangelical circles. You might say that I've almost seen it all. You see: I wasn't surprised, because gifted people are not always emotionally and relationally healthy people. The same principle is true for anointed people.

It takes emotionally and relationally healthy people to build healthy, transformed families that impact this world. Gifted, talented and even anointed people can build big ministries without being able to build healthy families.

In our travels we have been alarmed to see so many business and ministry leaders whose marriages and families were very dysfunctional. Some were even hanging on the precipice of tragedy. My dad used to always tell me, "For what profit is it to a man, if he gains the whole world, and loses his own soul?" (Matthew 16:26). It's so ironic to see corporate and ministry builders succumb; they lose their souls. (The *soul* in the Greek language represents your mind and emotions.) In their desire for glory, power, fame, money or even world impact, they lose their families, marriages, children and even their souls.

My wife Denise and I have not yet finished our journey to destiny. Although we are now in the empty nest phase, we are still learning, growing and adapting to these changes. We are still in the process of becoming healthy and whole in Christ. Even though we are still in process, I feel like we have acquired a few gems along the way. We've had the benefit of having friends and mentors who have shared their gems with us. Our church family has also played a very positive role in our family's transformation. We are forever grateful to God and to all of them.

This is why I have written this book: to spur you, to spark you, to come alongside you, to inspire you and to share our journey to destiny. May *The Transformed Family* help you experience your divine destiny.

CHAPTER 1

IT'S TIME FOR A BREAKTHROUGH

"He's just a chip off the old block."
"An apple doesn't fall far from the tree."
"Like father, like son."

These sayings have been around for a long, long time. There's nothing very hard to understand about them or the concepts to which they refer. They aren't controversial. They aren't original. They aren't surprising. After all, everyone knows that, for better or for worse, children usually resemble their parents.

Apparently it's not only English-speaking parents who have noticed this phenomenon, because similar maxims exist in other languages as well. In Spanish they say, "*de tal palo tal astilla,*" which means: "from such a stick such a splinter." In other words: The splinter will be like the stick from which it came. In French there is the phrase "*chasser du race,*" which means: "to run in the blood," or "to take after one's own kind." The Irish have a wealth of sayings regarding this subject. Two of those (translated to English) are: "How could the apple be, but as the apple tree?" and "What would the son of a cat do, but catch a mouse?" I would suspect that virtually every language has at least one saying that expresses the same reality, because it is not a cultural one, but a human one, a universal one and a biblical one.

Whether we are aware of it or not—and whether we intend to or not—we are continually passing on wisdom, knowledge, skills, morals, strengths and blessings to our children. We may also be passing on weaknesses, insecurities, deception, fear, bondage and even curses. The tremendous power we have to permanently impact our children's lives brings with it an equally tremendous responsibility. If, in ten or twenty years, we want to be happy with the results of our influence over our children, we would be well-advised to learn as much as possible about the principles behind this influence.

THE ROLE OF IMPARTATION IN PARENTING

The initial influence parents have over their children is physical. A newly-conceived child is already in possession of a staggering amount of genetic information, transferred to him or her from both parents. This will influence everything from the child's ultimate height, eye color and shoe size to his or her talents, intellect and basic temperament. The unborn child is further influenced by factors such as: the mother's physical well-being, her diet and whether she smokes, drinks alcohol or uses drugs during the pregnancy. During the pregnancy stage, the mother is the conduit of physical health and emotional well-being. Many studies have demonstrated the clear connection between the physical, emotional and relational well-being of the mother and unborn child.

After birth, the process of transfer continues. The interactions between mother, father, siblings, caretakers and child will foster the development of the core of the child's personality. Although a child cannot understand the environment that he or she is brought into, the child can feel and receive a massive influx of experiences, pictures and emotions that fill his or her mind, emotions and spirit. Even though a child cannot process or file all of those experiences, they have a profound impact on his or her emotional, intellectual, spiritual and relational development. A child will feel an environment that is tense, unloving, angry, nervous or anxious. This type of atmosphere can stunt a child's progress and leave him or her with scars that only Christ can erase. The purpose of this book is to help you create an atmosphere in your home that will facilitate a smooth transfer of all the blessings of heaven. You will notice in *The Transformed Family* that several words are used to describe this process of transformation or impartation. These terms, transformation and impartation, will be used interchangeably. Notice the concept of impartation in this Scripture:

Romans 1:11-12

*For I long to see you, that I may **impart** to you some spiritual gift, so that you may be established—that is: that I may be encouraged together with you by the mutual faith both of you and me.*

The Greek word used by Paul is "*metadidomi,*" which means "giving over that which I possess in abundance." In other words: Paul was saying that he had enough spiritual gifts to pass or transfer to the Romans. As parents, we, like Paul, can only give what we already have within us. Luke 6:45 reveals that *"out of the abundance of the heart his mouth speaks,"* which confirms this tendency. Moms and dads: If you are full of fear, you will, of course, pass on fear to your children. If you are full of faith, you will pass on faith. Paul noticed this fact in his relationship with Timothy.

2 Timothy 1:5

. . . when I call to remembrance the genuine faith that is in you, which dwelt first in your grandmother Lois and your mother Eunice, and I am persuaded is in you also.

Everything that is in us can and often will be passed on to our children. It is, therefore, our responsibility to decide what we want to impart and how we will do it. If the sins of the fathers are passed down three to four generations, then what about all the good, the blessings, the insights and wisdom that we have received from God? Can it be transferred successfully?

"Impartation" is the word I prefer to use when describing the act of transferring or passing on something from one human being to another. We can impart many things to many people in many ways, but in this book I will focus on impartation in the family: especially the process by which parents "give over" or transfer character traits and values to their children. The Bible has a great deal to say about impartation, in general and from parent to child, in particular.

Obstacles to Improvement

If impartation is real; its effects on our children are powerful and far-reaching. What might keep us from wanting to learn more about it? Why wouldn't we want to examine ourselves, with God's help, to find out just what it is we have to pass on to our children and how we can improve upon it? What would stop us from wanting to become more aware of how we are already imparting to them and work on perfecting our methods?

I believe there are four basic obstacles that might keep people from taking the first steps toward improving their parenting and impartation skills:

- **Pain**

It hurts to consider the connection between what we are and what our children are becoming. When we are confronted with it, we often feel guilty for every mistake and powerless to undo the damage.

- **Denial**

Denial is a more comfortable place to live. We fail even to acknowledge that problems exist, because reality is too unpleasant. Sometimes (1 Corinthians 13:12) *"we see in a mirror, dimly,"* because we choose to do so.

- **Fear**

Fear of failure can stop us from improving our situations, through the tools or techniques we have at our disposal. It seems safer to avoid trying at all than to try and fail. As children of God, however, we are called to be driven by a different engine.

2 Timothy 1:7
For God has not given us a spirit of fear, but of power and of love and of a sound mind.

- **Ignorance**

In Hosea 4:6 God said, *"My people are destroyed for lack of knowledge."* Sometimes we are simply ignorant of the things that could make us better imparters and better parents. After all, how many of us attended parenting classes before having children? The sad truth is that most people spend more time learning how to drive than how to parent.

The purpose of this book is to demolish all of the obstacles to improvement. It is my prayer that by the time you reach the end of this book you will be free from parental guilt, despair and fear. My desire is that you will no longer feel the need to live in denial and you will be equipped with the knowledge you need, in order to begin the process of becoming a parent who establishes a generational series of blessings. I encourage you to make a choice to change: a choice to break through and reach new levels for your family and for God.

CHAPTER 2

OVERCOMING THE FEAR OF FAILURE

The anguished cry of a parent wondering, "Where did I go wrong?" is so common it is almost cliché. All too many parents find themselves asking this question at one time or another. All too many even reach a point where they believe they are utter failures as parents. If you have been there or you are there right now, perhaps you can take a bit of comfort, knowing that you are not alone.

Feeling that one has failed as a mother or a father is not unique to contemporary parents. I'm sure it goes all the way back to Adam and Eve. (Imagine being the parents of the world's first murderer!) This feeling is not something that happens only to parents who have been negligent, lazy, uncaring or immoral. Often the moms and dads who end up wondering what went wrong are people who genuinely love God, have strong values, care deeply about their children and try hard to be good parents. I don't think that any of us ever set out to be awful parents. Most of us would do anything to help our children reach their God-given potential.

There are many cases in which parents do an excellent job with their children; nevertheless, one or more of them choose to rebel. Those parents can find hope in God's Word. The Word does not promise that properly trained children will never stray, but it does assure us that they will eventually return to the beliefs and values imparted to them when they were young.

Proverbs 22:6
Train a child in the way he should go,
and when he is old he will not depart from it.

On the other hand, there are some very godly people who truly do fail at parenting. Loving and serving God does not automatically make anyone a good spouse, nor does it automatically make anyone a good parent. Just as we must learn how to be good spouses, in order to have good marriages, we must also learn how to be good parents, in order to raise good children.

If you doubt this, just take a moment and consider the monumental failures of some Old Testament parents. David and Eli are two glaring examples of men who loved the Lord, but who raised ungodly children.

EXHIBIT ONE: KING DAVID
FATHERLY FAILURE

David was courageous, strong, full of faith, full of fire and a gifted, anointed leader. He had no trouble facing giants, commanding the respect of his troops or inspiring the admiration of his subjects. When it came to maintaining order and discipline under his own roof, he demonstrated an incredible lack of insight and strength.

When David's adult sons committed such crimes as rape, incest, murder and treason, he not only failed to carry out justice; he restrained others from doing so on his behalf. Why would a man with such passion for the Lord, such knowledge of and appreciation for God's laws, such love for his children and such valor in other aspects of his life have such a hard time disciplining his own offspring? Could it have something to do with David's own moral failure, when he committed adultery with Bathsheba and had her husband murdered? Perhaps David felt that his fall had stripped him of parental authority and robbed him of the right to demand a high code of conduct from his children. Perhaps he sensed that his family's respect for him had been replaced by contempt.

Whatever it was that weakened him, his lack of fatherly leadership only served to create more discord and rebellion. As a direct result, three of his favorite sons met with violent deaths. As much as we may admire David in other regards, none of us would want to imitate his parenting style.

EXHIBIT TWO: ELI
FATHERLY FAILURE WITH A SECOND CHANCE

We would also not want to turn out like Eli: the priest who failed miserably to raise children who loved and revered God. The Bible tells us:

1 Samuel 2:12
Now the sons of Eli were corrupt; they did not know the Lord.

Can you imagine the feelings of guilt and heartache Eli must have experienced when he thought about his two ungodly sons? Do you think that he tried harder with his young apprentice Samuel, because he had failed with his own children? Perhaps, by the time Samuel came along, Eli had had time to figure out where he went wrong with his sons and determined to avoid making the same mistakes with Samuel.

We need to acknowledge the part these fathers played in the failures of their children, so that we can learn from them. However, that doesn't mean we should be quick to blame parents when their children choose to rebel—especially when those children are old enough to distinguish between right and wrong and exercise control over their own behavior.

The Lord did not hold Eli responsible and chasten him directly for the wickedness of his sons; the Lord actually chastened Eli, because he had failed to restrain them. All children will disobey, test boundaries and may even rebel. God has made it clear, however, that parents who are soft on their children and indulge their disobedience are not doing so out of wise and loving concern:

Proverbs 13:24
He who spares his rod hates his son,
But he who loves him disciplines him promptly.

Furthermore, there is a special promise for those who are trained through proper discipline:

Hebrews 12:11
Now no chastening seems to be joyful for the present, but painful; nevertheless, afterward it yields the peaceable fruit of righteousness to those who have been trained by it.

If we read this passage of Scripture in context, we will see that the writer of Hebrews used the relationship between human parents and their children to illustrate a point about the relationship between God and His children. When we discipline our children, we can expect the same harvest of righteousness and peace. Incidentally, we can learn a great deal about raising children by observing the parenting techniques of our God: the best parent of all.

It has been said that God has no grandchildren. In other words: Being born to Christian parents does not automatically make one a member of God's family. We become His children by choice: not by the circumstances of our birth. To accept or reject Christ is a decision each person must make for himself or herself. Once our children decide to follow Christ, we cannot decide how faithful to Him they will be.

EXHIBIT THREE: JOB

Job 1:5
So it was, when the days of feasting had run their course, that Job would send and sanctify them, and he would rise early in the morning and offer burnt offerings according to the number of them all. For Job said, "It may be that my sons have sinned and cursed God in their hearts." Thus Job did regularly.

Job seemed to have some real doubts that his children were living out a vibrant faith in God. Job made extra sacrifices, just in case. He may have raised them to love God, but was unsure if they had followed through. Ultimately, each one of us is responsible and accountable to God for our actions, choices, decisions and lifestyles. Even those of us who had terrible parents cannot forever use them to justify our bad behavior. At some point, each of us must repent of our own sins and forgive those who have hurt us. We must then allow God to heal us, transform us and teach us how to live.

If people aren't supposed to spend their lives blaming parents for their own mistakes, does that mean parents have nothing to do with how their children turn out? Absolutely not! Each parent plays a huge role in the life of his or her child and, at every stage of the child's development there are many things the parent can do, that will have a powerful effect on the outcome. We must never underestimate the impact we have on our children. God designed us to have great influence and authority over our children—and He expects us to use both wisely.

CHANGE IS POSSIBLE

Philippians 4:13
I can do all things through Christ who strengthens me.

Perhaps you are one of those parents who is now asking, "Where did I go wrong?" Maybe you're at the point where you believe you're a complete failure as a parent. On the other hand, you may feel that you're doing pretty well, but you know there's always room for improvement. No matter how we think we rate as parents, we can begin right now, to make a change for the better. We begin by asking God to change us into what He wants us to be and cooperate with Him, as He answers that prayer, so that we will have something worthwhile to pass on to our children.

As you progress through this book you will learn new ways to impart truth, honor, character and anointing to your children. As you put these truths into action, I believe you will begin to see amazing results in your children.

I encourage you to not allow guilt or shame to stop you from learning more about creating a healthy family with successful children. The only purpose of guilt is to lead us to the cross, in sincere repentance, so that we can then walk away forgiven and cleansed: ready to begin anew with restored hope, peace and joy in abundance.

Take a few minutes at the cross and leave your burdens there at the feet of Jesus. It is not His will for us to carry the weight of guilt and shame for the rest of our lives. God will forgive all of our parental shortcomings. There is no failure so great that it cannot be forgiven and repaired by God. It is never too late to put our lives and our loved ones into God's hands. It is never too late to start over and change what and how we impart. God is not limited by our past and He is not limited by time. Even if our children are grown, it is not too late to change the course of the next generation.

Isaiah 1:18
"Come now, and let us reason together,"
Says the LORD,
"Though your sins are like scarlet

They shall be as white as snow;
Though they are red like crimson,
They shall be as wool."

Pray this prayer to begin your road to parental recovery:

"DEAR LORD JESUS, I LOVE YOU AND I NEED YOU. PLEASE FORGIVE ME FOR ALL OF MY WEAKNESSES, SINS AND FAILURES. MAY YOUR MERCY AND GRACE FILL MY LIFE, MY RELATIONSHIPS, MY MATE AND MY CHILDREN. I WANT TO START OVER WITH YOU AS THE CENTER OF OUR HOME. JESUS, TAKE THE WHEEL OF OUR FAMILY. I HAND OVER CONTROL TO THE HOLY SPIRIT. HAVE YOUR WAY IN MY LIFE AND THE LIFE OF MY FAMILY."

Questions to Make You Think

Q: What family habits or strongholds need to be addressed at this time in your life?

Q: What force has hindered you from leading your family into a season of transformation?

Q: Why would people like David and Job experience family challenges?

Chapter 3

Success Is Possible

The life of Timothy proves that parents can be successful. In his second letter to Timothy the apostle Paul cites a beautiful example of parental impartation in the life of his young protégé:

2 Timothy 1:5
...when I call to remembrance the genuine faith that is in you, which dwelt first in your grandmother Lois and your mother Eunice, and I am persuaded is in you also.

As any devout mother or grandmother would have done, these women must have spent many hours instructing Timothy in the faith. They probably told him many of the same Bible stories children still love to hear today: the stories of how God created the world and everything in it; how He kept Noah, his family and the animals safe and dry inside the ark, while it rained for forty days and forty nights; how He helped a little shepherd boy defeat a mighty giant with just a slingshot and a pebble.

Surely they taught him to love, fear and obey the Lord. Perhaps they helped him memorize portions of Scripture, taught him to sing the psalms and reminded him to say his prayers at bedtime. It's almost certain that they told him about the promised Messiah and passed along to him the hope that, even in Timothy's lifetime, the great Deliverer might come.

If Lois and Eunice were successful transferring their faith, it is most likely because they accompanied their words with actions. Timothy had opportunities to see them living out their faith day after day and year after year. Certainly, words of instruction can be valuable tools, but they are weak and ineffective if we do not back them up with good examples. "Do as I say, not as I do" has never been a good parenting philosophy.

GIVE WHAT YOU HAVE

Never forget this principle of transference: "You cannot give what you do not have." You can only give what you have. I have over 28 years of experience as a counselor, pastor and leader. I've discovered that the next generation is generally much greater than their parents or they are much worse. It seems like the pattern of Elijah and Elisha is very common in modern day situations. Elisha was the spiritual son of Elijah. Elisha loved what his mentor and coach stood for. So, when Elijah was going to die, Elisha asked Elijah for a double portion. In other words: He really liked what he saw. So, he wanted twice as much. Do your children admire, love and respect you? Do you think that they would want twice as much of your spirit? If you summarized the content of your spirit, what would it look like? If you could evaluate your spirit, attitude and faith, what grade would you give yourself? (For example: 0 = horrible, depressed, depraved; 10 = a saint and an inspiration) If your children had two times the condition of your spirit, would that be a good or bad thing?

In Timothy's case, he was inspired, not by his non-believing, Greek father, but by his believing mom and grandmother. How attractive is your faith to your children? The lives of Lois and Eunice must have looked pretty amazing to Timothy. Don't forget that being a Christian was a dangerous proposition to embrace in the first century. Timothy chose the hardest, riskiest path. He must have seen something in mom and grandma to make it worth the risk. Was it what they said or what they did?

Although we are unsure of what methods Lois and Eunice used to transfer their faith, we know that they groomed Timothy for greatness. Their training made him wise beyond his years and laid a firm foundation for continued impartation and personal growth. The apostle Paul recognized this young man who was ready for an adventure of a lifetime. Timothy was ready for more impartation. All the work of Lois and Eunice paid off. They had prepared him to become a history-maker. Are you preparing your children to become history-makers? Do they believe in God? Is their faith firmly founded in a real and powerful God? Are they hungry for more of the Holy Spirit?

ACTIONS SPEAK LOUDER THAN WORDS

Someone has said that "what we allow, we teach." Here's an illustration: A dad who took the time to instruct his son on the basics of financial responsibility—tithing, saving, avoiding debt—but caved in right away, when the boy begged for an advance on his allowance, in order to buy a game that he just couldn't wait to have.

Another illustration is this: A mother with two preschool-aged children who ran wild through a restaurant, while she finished her coffee. In a weak, whining voice, she periodically asked them to sit down and be quiet, but never actually forced the children to comply. Another example is this: A couple who have warned their teenagers about the dangers of movies and video games that feature graphic violence, sex or occult themes, but looked the other way when the kids brought home some of the very items they were cautioned about.

In each of those illustrations, the children learned exactly the opposite of what the parents intended to teach. How can that be? Well, if you give children a rule or a lesson, but fail to enforce it or live it out, they will simply learn that you don't mean what you say. If a child has to decide between believing what you say or believing what you demonstrate, he or she will almost invariably believe the latter. Do your actions speak louder than your words?

IMPARTATION OF TRUTH OR PRINCIPLES
IS MORE READILY CAUGHT THAN TAUGHT.

Our children learn primarily by what they see, feel and absorb from their environment. Our words are either confirmed and illustrated by our actions or contradicted and weakened by them. We may not be out rightly explaining anything to our children, lecturing them, rewarding them or even disciplining them, but we are constantly training them. What are we teaching them through our words, examples, priorities and reactions? The answer to this question is important, because it has eternal repercussions.

WHAT SEEDS ARE YOU SOWING?

There is no doubt that we are constantly pouring into our children, but what are we filling them with? Can you identify some of the elements that you have accidentally or purposefully poured into them? There will come a time when it cannot help but overflow with whatever we have been putting into it. You are sowing many things into your kids: not all of them good and not all of them bad. We need to be aware of this fact, because someday we will have to harvest the consequences. We should remember Galatians 6:7, no matter how uneasy it may sometimes make us feel: *"Do not be deceived, God is not mocked; for whatever a man sows, that he will also reap."*

The truth of the sowing and reaping principle is most obvious in families. It is not a coincidence that problems in a home are often passed on to the following generations. As a counselor and pastor, I have witnessed, firsthand, the reality of generational curses. Alcoholism, violence, ignorance, poor self-esteem, prejudice, obesity and countless other, personal problems are passed from parent to child. This fact is a given in the medical and mental-health fields. It is not a coincidence that the review of a patient's family history is an important part of any visit to a doctor, counselor or psychologist.

This universal truth is crucial to understand: Each of us have been given gifts and liabilities by our families. Our parents, grandparents, aunts, uncles and siblings all impart into our lives. Although we are not mere products of our environment—or our genetics, for that matter—we are impacted by them in many ways. Recognizing those who have poured into us and what has been poured into us will help us, in turn, make choices that are deliberate, insightful and strategic.

As I review my own childhood, I've realized what good was poured into me and I've made a conscious effort to take this foundation to my children. The foundation of every healthy home should be honor, respect and love. Let's take a few moments to develop these foundations.

RESPECT FOR AUTHORITY

At times our role as parents is simply to prepare our children, so that they will be able to receive impartation from others. We are the ones who teach them to respect or disrespect pastors, teachers, coaches and employers. This is, indeed, a crucial role. How can children receive anything from a leader if you have taught them to disrespect those in leadership? Respect is a principle that my wife Denise and I have made a special effort to instill in our children. It includes teaching them such simple things as how they are to address those in authority. (For example: "Mr. Smith" instead of "Bill," "Mrs. Jones" instead of "Sue" and "Pastor John" instead of "Hey, you.")

Of course, as we just mentioned, children learn best by example. Our children will respect authority figures no more than we do. If we grumble about our bosses, argue with our children's teachers, complain about the principals of their schools, make dishonest excuses when a police officer pulls us over for speeding, ridicule elected officials whenever we read magazines or criticize the pastors, worship leaders and Sunday school teachers of our churches, we shouldn't be surprised when our children begin to rebel against authority. They are simply following in our footsteps.

God has promised that we will reap what we sow. If we want our children to respect and honor us, we must train them by word and by example, to respect and honor others. Can you imagine what would happen if we began to disciple our children while they were still very small? By the time they reached high school, they would be ready to withstand the power of peer pressure and to change their campuses for Christ.

How many of us, as Christian parents, fail to pour our faith into our children? If we suspect we are failing in this way, we need to take a hard look at ourselves and ask, "Where does the problem lie? Is it in my faith or in my ability to pour out to my child? Have I demonstrated the principle of honor and respect to my children?" Let's not forget that the first commandment that carries a blessing with it is as follows:

Exodus 20:12
"Honor your father and your mother, that your days may be long upon the land which the LORD your God is giving you."

RESPECT AND HONOR IN THE HOME

Success is possible for parents, as we prioritize the concept of respect and honor in our homes. I've listed seven steps that can help your family establish the cornerstone of a strong family:

1. As parents, let's take a moment to ask God to forgive us for any disrespect or dishonor that we have been guilty of.
2. Begin to demonstrate respect to your parents, grandparents and other authority figures.
3. Always speak well of your mate in front of your children. If you are in a conflict with your mate, confront privately.
4. Do not allow critical talk about other authority figures. If there is a conflict, help your children resolve it in a biblical fashion.
5. Create an environment of respect and honor in your home. Look for opportunities to illustrate or practice love and respect, on a daily basis.
6. Teach your children to respect and honor teachers, coaches and other adult leaders.
7. Demonstrate love.

1 Corinthians 13:3
And though I bestow all my goods to feed the poor, and though I give my body to be burned, but have not love, it profits me nothing.

1 Corinthians 13:13
And now abide faith, hope, love, these three; but the greatest of these is love.

Honor and respect set a beautiful foundation for a healthy home, but love must be the cornerstone. The Bible is clear: *"And though I have the gift of prophecy and understand all mysteries and all knowledge, and though I have all faith, so that I could remove mountains, but have not love, I am nothing"* (1 Corinthians 13:2). John the beloved reveals the following:

1 John 4:20-21
If someone says, "I love God" and hates his brother, he is a liar: for he who does not love his brother whom he has seen, how can he love God whom he has not seen? And this commandment we have from Him: that he who loves God must love his brother also.

Moms and dads, this should be your priority and daily prayer: "God, help me love like You love. Help me love my mate as You do. Help me love my children as the Father does. I need Your help. May unconditional love fill every one of us more and more. Amen." Paul prayed this prayer:

Philippians 1:9
And this I pray, that your love may abound still more and more in knowledge and all discernment . . .

Only God can help our homes be full of love, honor and respect.

FOUNDATIONS OF A HEALTHY HOME

Have you ever prioritized the qualities that you want to pass on to your children? Have you succeeded in imparting a living, vibrant faith to your children? Have you succeeded in transferring the same morals and standards that you have embraced? Earlier we looked at Old Testament examples of godly parents who failed to pass on their faith to their children. Can you think of a few contemporary, Christian leaders who also have failed in this area?

You may have heard the stereotypes about preachers' kids or "PKs." Perhaps, in reference to a pastor's child who was behaving badly, you've heard someone say, "Oh, all PKs act that way!" Denise and I have chosen not to let this myth discourage us or affect the way we relate to our children. In fact, we diligently pray for our kids, pray over our kids, model our faith for them and train them in the faith. All this does not mean, however, that we haven't had our ups and downs.

Before my dad passed away, I took time to discover and write down the qualities that I inherited from him and my mom. I've listed more references to my dad, because I struggled so much to discover them. You see: My dad and I didn't have a great relationship when I was young. I always thought that my mom "hung the moon." In my mind, she was a saint. My dad, on the other hand, had a few rough edges, which I struggled with. In fact, for a while I had so much anger toward him that I lost sight of all the good that he tried to demonstrate to me. I don't blame him for my failure to see the good; the fault was mine. Through prayer and the love of my heavenly Father, I was able to find the treasures that had been hidden under all the garbage. I hope that they resonate in your life as they did in mine.

HONESTY AND INTEGRITY

I am sure that all of you want your children to be honest. I learned this from my dad. He worked for a large corporation and had access to company resources, but refused to use anything for personal needs, from pens to the company car. My father was very conscientious about not taking advantage of his position.

LOYALTY

My father demonstrated this characteristic by his fierce loyalty to his company. In our home, we could never use tissues other than those made by his company. In fact, in the '70s, it became common to say a particular brand name when one wanted a tissue. However, in our home, we could not refer to tissues by competitors names. It may sound insignificant, but I learned loyalty from this practice.

GUARDING THE TONGUE

Many families have a habit of speaking ill of others. Family meals often become times of gossip, slander, backbiting and fault-finding. I will never forget the voice of my father saying, "Paul, if you don't have anything nice to say, then don't say anything at all." It was forbidden to speak ill of others in our home.

HARD WORK

The Bible says:

Proverbs 24:30-34
I went by the field of the lazy man,
And by the vineyard of the man devoid of understanding;
And there it was, all overgrown with thorns;
Its surface was covered with nettles;
Its stone wall was broken down.
When I saw it, I considered it well;
I looked on it and received instruction:
A little sleep, a little slumber,
A little folding of the hands to rest;

So shall your poverty come like a prowler,
And your need like an armed man.

What a great admonition for us, as parents! How can we instill a great work ethic in our homes? There's only one way: by working hard and seeing to it that our children do the same. Every one of these qualities that are modeled, taught and reinforced will become part of who they are. My dad worked so hard and it inspired me.

Positive Outlook on Life

It was while the apostle Paul was a prisoner in Rome that he wrote the famous words: *"I can do all things through Christ who strengthens me"* (Philippians 4:13). His positive outlook on life obviously had nothing to do with his circumstances. Neither did my mom's. It was she who best demonstrated this quality in our family and passed it on to her children. She has been like the unsinkable Molly Brown. During her life she has faced many trials, but she kept a wonderful attitude throughout. Even though she is now in her 80s and just recently lost her husband of over 50 years, her desire to learn, grow and touch the lives of others continues to move her forward for God.

Recently my mom suffered a terrible fall and two strokes, yet she has responded like a true champion. Due to the physical setback, she was forced to leave her two bedroom apartment, that she shared with my dad for many years. She moved into an apartment for seniors, where she can still live with independence, but enjoy the company of other seniors on a daily basis. At 87, she moved across the hall from a high school friend named Gerry. They have so much fun together. They have even started a ministry to Alzheimer's patients. Gerry plays the piano and my mom sings and loves it. Wow! My mom is like Caleb. My mom really has 50/20 vision. Do you know what 50/20 vision is? I found that verse in Genesis 50:20. It is the attitude that helped determine Joseph's success.

Genesis 50:20

"But as for you, you meant evil against me, but God meant it for good, in order to bring it about as it is this day, to save many people alive."

You might say his attitude determined his altitude: his ability to rise above the circumstances. When my Isabelle had cancer at the age of eighteen, she too displayed this unbeatable attitude. She even played college basketball after her treatments. Prior to her wonderful healing, God also gave me this attitude, as He dropped Romans 8:28 into my mind at a really difficult time, during Isabelle's treatment:

And we know that all things work together for good to those who love God, to those who are the called according to His purpose.

What the enemy meant to kill my daughter and destroy us, God was going to use for good: the saving of many souls. My daughter's miracle has gone around the world and touched countless lives.

MOMS AND DADS, TEACH YOUR CHILDREN TO REBOUND FROM ADVERSITY.

There are many more truths that were passed down to my siblings and I. I am forever indebted to my parents and my older brothers and sisters. I was the fifth child to watch and learn from this family environment. Parents, I repeat: Never downplay the effect of impartation in your home. What your children see and perceive in the home will become more real than anything else they experience.

Questions to Make You Think

Q: What do you want to pass on to your children?

Q: What have you learned from your parents that has helped you?

Q: What are the foundations of your family?

Q: How can you add more love, respect and honor into your home?

CHAPTER 4

SUCCESSFUL PARENTING: THE STRATEGY

The Old Testament is full of examples and guidelines for parenting. Jewish traditions laid the responsibility of teaching and imparting squarely on the shoulders of the parents.

Deuteronomy 6:6-9
"And these words which I command you today shall be in your heart. You shall teach them diligently to your children, and shall talk of them when you sit in your house, when you walk by the way, when you lie down, and when you rise up. You shall bind them as a sign on your hand, and they shall be as frontlets between your eyes. You shall write them on the doorposts of your house and on your gates."

Some parents believe the primary responsibility for their child's spiritual instruction belongs to the local church. The preceding verses clearly demonstrate that an hour or two of Sunday school, once a week, is not enough. Children need to be continually immersed in God's Word, so that it becomes as natural as breathing. This is especially important in today's society, where all of us are constantly pummeled by ungodly influences.

However this does not mean we have to preach to our children around the clock or quote a new Scripture verse every few minutes. Christian instruction can be as simple as taking a walk in the park and pointing out all the beautiful things the Lord has made for us to enjoy, singing along with your favorite Christian CDs (as you do household chores together) or leading your child in a quick prayer for God's help, when he or she confides in you about a problem. Later on in this book we will suggest other, easy ways to instruct and impart to your children.

DEVELOP YOUR STRATEGY

Solomon was the first son of his mother Bathsheba and her husband David. We all know the story of David's murderous lust for this bathing beauty. Can you imagine the impact this must have had on Solomon? His dad stole his mom away from her first husband. Wow. That's quite a beginning, wasn't it? Perhaps the tragic background caused Solomon to seek God in a very personal way. The book of Proverbs is a testament to his desire to lay a firm foundation for his own children. We can learn some important truths from him, that will help us become parents of kings and queens.

- **Strategy: Solomon honored his father David.**

Proverbs 4:1-5
Hear, my children, the instruction of a father,
And give attention to know understanding;
For I give you good doctrine:
Do not forsake my law.
When I was my father's son,
Tender and the only one in the sight of my mother,
He also taught me, and said to me:

"Let your heart retain my words;
Keep my commands, and live.
Get wisdom! Get understanding!
Do not forget, nor turn away from the words of my mouth."

You can certainly recognize Solomon's sincere desire to impart pearls of wisdom to his sons.

- **Strategy: Solomon was committed to transferring a hunger to become wise and demonstrate understanding.**

Proverbs 5:1
My son, pay attention to my wisdom;
lend your ear to my understanding . . .

James 1:5
If any of you lacks wisdom, let him ask of God, who gives to all liberally and without reproach, and it will be given to him.

- **Strategy: Solomon honored his wife's role in parenting.** Notice that he mentions the mother's role in parenting.

Proverbs 1:8
My son, hear the instruction of your father,
And do not forsake the law of your mother . . .

Some people believe it's primarily the mother's job to teach her children about spiritual and moral matters. In these verses, however, Solomon makes it clear that a child needs to receive instruction and teaching from both mother and father.

- **Strategy: Moses laid a foundation of parenting for Solomon.**

Exodus 20:4-6
"You shall not make for yourself a carved image—any likeness of anything that is in heaven above, or that is in the earth beneath, or that is

in the water under the earth; you shall not bow down to them nor serve them. For I, the LORD your God, am a jealous God, visiting the iniquity of the fathers upon the children to the third and fourth generations of those who hate Me, but showing mercy to thousands, to those who love Me and keep My commandments."

Solomon's teaching can be interpreted in the light of Exodus 20:4-6. He realized the massive, generational consequences of his parenting approach. He did his best to teach his children the benefits of seeking wisdom and understanding. Sadly, however, his life choices undermined a kingdom that splintered after his death.

- **Strategy: Ask God for mercy and grace.**

We must call upon God's mercy. What can we learn from Solomon's life and legacy? Have we learned that good intentions do not guarantee good results? Have we learned that we need the grace and mercy of God to pour over our families? When we dedicate our children to God, we are asking Him to help us and help our children. We must invite the Lord to come alongside us and help us teach our children. All our efforts are in vain without the power and guidance of the Holy Spirit. He is the One who will convict of sin, draw our children to Himself, fill them, enable them to follow Him, and give them peace through all of life's challenges.

- **Strategy: We can touch generations through our children and grandchildren.**

Deuteronomy 4:9
"Only take heed to yourself, and diligently keep yourself, lest you forget the things your eyes have seen, and lest they depart from your heart all the days of your life. And teach them to your children and your grandchildren . . ."

We must diligently and gratefully remember all that God has done for us, in us and through us—never allowing our love for Him to grow cold and never taking Him for granted. This is the only way we can hope to pass on a rich and glorious, spiritual inheritance to our children and grandchildren. Let us not just hope for children who love God; let us teach them and show them how to live righteously. My wife and I recently became grandparents for the first time. We are having the time of our lives. Denise has bought clothes and toys for young Luke on almost every shopping trip. Both of us look for opportunities to baby-sit or simply spend time with him. (He calls us Nana and Papa.) We are so in love with our next generation. Many times during worship, he has joined us on stage, to be with his Papa and Nana. He loves the worship and we are training him to be comfortable in front of a crowd. Luke's training started the day he left his mother's womb.

As soon as he is old enough, we will expose him to missions, helping the poor and serving his community. His parents are doing such a great job raising him. Denise and I feel honored to be involved in their lives. I have often expressed a desire to encourage our children and grandchildren to climb on our shoulders and to go further than we have ever gone for God. Is this your desire as well?

A PRECIOUS LEGACY

Perhaps the Old Testament teachings hold the secrets to the strength and resilience of the Jewish people. They show us how, in spite of continual persecution, repeated attempts to exterminate them and centuries of dispersion (usually without a nation they could call home) the Jewish people have been able to survive. The principles are divinely designed to create a strong family identity and a valuable legacy. By putting them into effect, the Jewish people have effectively transferred (imparted) their faith and their traditions, from generation to generation. Their very survival as a people has depended on their ability to practice impartation in the home. If God's principles of impartation helped hold the Jewish people together, in the midst of trying circumstances, what effect do you think they might have upon your family?

STRATEGY: GREAT COMMUNICATION IS CRUCIAL

Recently Josh McDowell was a special guest speaker at a city-wide church school conference, hosted by our church. It was exciting to see this great, Christian apologist who made such an impact on me in my early days as a believer. He first won my respect and gratitude, as the author of *Evidence That Demands a Verdict*—a book that gave me a firm foundation for my faith in Jesus Christ. As a new Christian, dealing with the challenges of college life, that was pivotal.

I found his talks at the conference refreshing and rewarding. Among other things, he spoke of the "six A's" of communicating with our children. These points are a sort of road map that can help us begin to enter our child's world. I have borrowed McDowell's "six A's," along with my own applications and suggestions for implementation:

AFFIRMATION

Romans 12:15
Rejoice with those who rejoice, and weep with those who weep.

To affirm means to validate, support, sustain or uphold. I will never forget counseling a man, in regard to his rebellious, teenage son. As we talked, I realized that this man had nothing good to say about him. I asked the father to try to find something of value in his child, but he was only able to see weaknesses. I had no trouble finding many redeeming qualities in the young man and found it disturbing and sad that his father couldn't. The son's rebellion was, in part, a reaction to a rejecting father who could never be pleased.

Affirmation is the bridge that connects us to our children. Find the good in your children and let them know what you see. Validate their likes and dislikes, as well as their thoughts and feelings. Reward them for their accomplishments and verbally acknowledge their good efforts.

ACCEPTANCE

Romans 15:7 (NIV)

Accept one another, then, just as Christ accepted you, in order to bring praise to God.

Can you accept your children, even if they are different from you? Can you step into their world and make them feel loved, no matter what they do? McDowell mentioned that acceptance creates a sense of security in a child. I agree. Acceptance is very similar to God's *agape* love: unconditional, unchanging and absolutely dependable. We should acknowledge our children's positive traits and behavior, but we shouldn't give them the impression that those are the reasons we love them. They need to know that our love is not a result of their good performance or charming qualities. If it were, that would mean we would cease to love them the moment they stopped performing well or being charming. We must let our children know we love them, simply because they exist and simply because they are our children.

APPRECIATION

Matthew 3:17
And suddenly a voice came from heaven, saying, "This is My beloved Son, in whom I am well pleased."

One of my favorite books on personal development is *Search for Significance* by Robert McGee. I encourage all of you to read this book and to have your child read the teen version, as soon as they are old enough. McGee underlines four obstacles to a person's sense of significance: fear of failure, fear of rejection, fear of punishment and shame. McDowell also spoke about a sense of significance and emphasized the important role of appreciation in helping our children develop it. If the only way we demonstrate appreciation to our children is by thanking them when they set the table or take out the trash, we are not doing a great deal to enhance their sense of significance. Although we should express appreciation for what they do, it is even more important to express appreciation for *them*, for who they are.

Furthermore: We should consider all that appreciation means and apply it to our children in its fullest sense. The fourth edition of *Webster's New World College Dictionary* tells us that *to appreciate*, among other things, is "to think well of; to understand and enjoy; to esteem; to recognize and be grateful for; and to estimate the quality or worth of," in a favorable sense. If we put McDowell's and McGee's approaches together, we will find many ways to help our children overcome the obstacles to a sense of significance, by expressions of appreciation and other types of verbal reinforcement:

Fear of failure: The remedy for this is to appreciate the effort, not the outcome. A parent with this attitude makes comments like: "Just do your best. That's all I want to see," or "I don't love you more when you win or less when you lose. What I care about is that you give it your best shot."

Fear of rejection: To combat this fear, reinforce unconditional acceptance and love with comments like, "Son, you are forgiven for what you did. I love you so much and I appreciate your honesty."

Fear of punishment: Fight the fear of punishment by exercising fair and consistent discipline in love, clarifying the motivation behind the discipline with words like, "Honey, I am not disciplining you because I am angry. I am disciplining you because I love you and care about you." There is a big difference between discipline and punishment.

Shame: Get rid of shame by helping your children realize that failing does not mean they are failures. Say something like, "You may be feeling really bad about yourself right now, but you're still just as special to us as ever. You're a great kid and we're so thankful to be your parents." You might also say, "Sweetheart, it's never too late to make a fresh start. God is the God of second chances. All of us fail sometimes, but God's love and my love for you can overcome anything." There are times when I have even shared about my own failings, as well as explaining my choice to receive God's forgiveness and to forgive myself.

AFFECTION

1 John 4:7
Beloved, let us love one another, for love is of God; and everyone who loves is born of God and knows God.

In a cruel, sex-crazed world, filled with twisted notions about love and relationships, wholesome, verbal and physical affection are like warm blankets on a cold day, or like safe harbors in a storm. More than ever, our children need pure, healthy expressions of genuine love and tenderness. In fact, this need is present in all of us.

In a few of his letters, the apostle Paul encouraged the saints to greet each other with a "holy kiss." Take time to hug and kiss your kids every day, no matter how old they are. Verbally repeat to them how wonderful they are. I am very affectionate with my three kids. I love to hold their hands, hug them and say affectionate words to them. On occasion, I even sing love songs to them. Why not? The Bible tells us that our heavenly Father sings over us:

Zephaniah 3:17
"The LORD your God in your midst,
The Mighty One, will save;
He will rejoice over you with gladness,
He will quiet you with His love,
He will rejoice over you with singing."

AVAILABILITY

Matthew 19:13-15
Then little children were brought to Him that He might put His hands on them and pray, but the disciples rebuked them. But Jesus said, "Let the little children come to Me, and do not forbid them; for of such is the kingdom of heaven." And He laid His hands on them and departed from there.

In Gary Chapman's book *The Five Love Languages* (which I highly recommend), he teaches couples how to determine their preferred means of communicating and receiving love. The theory is that, if we don't learn to express love for our mates in their preferred language(s), they may intellectually know that we love them, but will never truly feel loved. For example: If my wife's love language was "quality time," she would feel emotionally starved if I never got around to spending any quality time with her, even if I sent her beautiful gifts and told her how much I love her, several times a day.

According to Chapman, the five love languages are: **touch, acts of service, quality time, gifts and words of affirmation.** Of course, we may appreciate and understand all the love languages to certain degrees, but one or two of the languages will speak much more clearly to our hearts than others. It can make many of us feel loved, just knowing that someone is making the effort to figure out what our love language is and speak it to us!

I believe that our children also have love languages. There are keys that can open their hearts and help them feel loved. In our family, one of our girls loves to be held and loves words of affirmation. She is a romantic, tender-hearted, young woman. Our other daughter is a little gem who doesn't like the touchy-feely stuff; acts of service and gifts are what make her feel loved. My son looks for quality time, touch and encouraging words to fill up his love tank.

What is your love language? What love languages do your children best understand? "Availability" may not be one of Chapman's five love languages, but it is one that speaks volumes to most children. Virtually all of them will appreciate it if you are physically and emotionally available to them. Jesus had a very busy schedule and was surrounded by people with urgent needs; yet, he managed to make time for children. How about you? Are you available to your children?

ACCOUNTABILITY

Romans 14:12
So then each of us will give an account of himself to God.

If we want to raise healthy adults, we must insist that our children be accountable to us. Yes, that's what I meant to say: adults. Our goal as parents goes beyond raising healthy children. We want our children to become healthy adults and productive members of society. We want them to resist temptation and make great decisions for their lives. As Christians, we want them to love and serve God with all of their hearts, to bear much fruit while here on earth and, ultimately, to make it to heaven. These goals will not be achieved unless we impart wisdom, understanding and knowledge to our children—and unless we keep them accountable. **Accountability includes reasoning, disciplining, goal-setting and following up.** God, Himself, did this with Israel:

Isaiah 1:18-20
"Come now, let us reason together,"
says the LORD.
"Though your sins are like scarlet,
they shall be as white as snow;
though they are red as crimson,
they shall be like wool.
If you are willing and obedient,
you will eat the best from the land;
but if you resist and rebel,
you will be devoured by the sword;"
For the mouth of the LORD has spoken.

The well-known public-service announcement that announces the time, then asks, "Do you know where your children are?" That is a prime example of accountability. Ask questions, know your children's friends and activities, set boundaries, enforce reasonable curfews, reward and discipline your children.

Questions to Make You Think

Q: What is your strategy to establish your children and grandchildren?

Q: What teaching of Solomon has helped you the most as a parent?

Q: Do you think about future generations? Are you laying the foundation for those generations?

Q: How will you help your children and grandchildren climb on your shoulders to go further for God?

Q: What is your love language? What are your spouses?

Q: What are your children's love languages?

CHAPTER 5

THE POWER TO BLESS

The power to bless is a truth that can unlock your child's destiny. It is, in many ways, both prophetic and creative. The blessing has been a tool that God has used in His relationship with mankind for generations. In Genesis we see Him bless Adam and Eve.

Genesis 1:22
And God blessed them, saying, "Be fruitful and multiply, and fill the waters in the seas, and let birds multiply on the earth."

Later on in Genesis, Abraham is blessed by God. This blessing was a seed blessing for the birth of faith, through an obedient man.

Genesis 14:19-20
And he blessed him and said:
"Blessed be Abram of God Most High,
Possessor of heaven and earth;
And blessed be God Most High,
Who has delivered your enemies into your hand."
And he gave him a tithe of all.

In Genesis, Jacob was blessed to birth the nation of Israel.

Genesis 28:14

"Also, your descendants shall be as the dust of the earth; you shall spread abroad to the west and the east, to the north and the south; and in you and in your seed all the families of the earth shall be blessed."

The power to bless is just as important to you and I. Our words of blessing serve as a tool to impart and help our children reach their potential. The concept of impartation and the transference of morals, character and spirit in the home can be found deeply intertwined in the Hebrew culture. Jacob, for example, believed strongly in the impartation of a special, one-time, patriarchal (traditionally bestowed upon a firstborn son) blessing, through the laying on of hands and a prayer from the father. He was willing to risk the wrath of both his older brother Esau and their father Isaac, in order to obtain it. Jacob (whose name means "deceiver" and "supplanter") took advantage of the failing eyesight of his dying father and tricked his way into receiving the blessing rightly belonging to Esau.

Genesis 27:18-24

So he went to his father and said, "My father."
And he said, "Here I am. Who are you, my son?"
Jacob said to his father, "I am Esau your firstborn; I have done just as you told me; please arise, sit and eat of my game, that your soul may bless me."
But Isaac said to his son, "How is it that you have found it so quickly, my son?"
And he said, "Because the LORD your God brought it to me."
Isaac said to Jacob, "Please come near, that I may feel you, my son, whether you are really my son Esau or not." So Jacob went near to Isaac his father, and he felt him and said, "The voice is Jacob's voice, but the hands are the hands of Esau." And he did not recognize him,

because his hands were hairy like his brother Esau's hands; so he blessed him.
Then he said, "Are you really my son Esau?"
He said, "I am."

There was no transference of land or titles through this blessing. The birthright of the firstborn did carry with it a double-portion of the inheritance, but Esau had already, voluntarily forfeited that for a bowl of stew. I know that this sounds absurd, but it perfectly illustrates the fact that Esau did not value the birthright. He couldn't wait for his dad's death. He wanted instant gratification. This demonstrates that Esau placed no value on the birthright or parental blessing, but Jacob was willing to do anything to get it.

Genesis 25:29-34
Now Jacob cooked a stew; and Esau came in from the field, and he was weary. And Esau said to Jacob, "Please feed me with that same red stew, for I am weary." Therefore his name was called Edom. But Jacob said, "Sell me your birthright as of this day." And Esau said, "Look, I am about to die; so what is this birthright to me?" Then Jacob said, "Swear to me as of this day." So he swore to him, and sold his birthright to Jacob. And Jacob gave Esau bread and stew of lentils; then he ate and drank, arose, and went his way. Thus Esau despised his birthright.

JACOB WANTED THE BIRTHRIGHT AND THE BLESSING

Jacob wanted the birthright and the blessing, because he believed in the power of both. After he received the birthright from the short-sighted Esau, he set his desire on the blessings. Why was he still so anxious to receive the blessing? What was he after? As things turned out, legal rights notwithstanding, Jacob never did actually receive the double-portion of Isaac's property. As we continue to read about and consider Jacob's life, it seems less and less likely that he was simply looking for material wealth. There was something greater—something more significant—that he longed for: a supernatural blessing.

A Contemporary Father's Blessing

Although I was not raised in the Hebrew culture, the fatherly blessing was a very important, annual event in our home. Each New Year's Day, all the Goulet children would gather together with our mother and father, in order to celebrate this family tradition. One by one we were ushered into a separate room. I can remember so clearly how it felt to kneel in front of my parents and hear those words of blessing from my father. I loved it. It made me feel honored, accepted and embraced by my parents. None of us were born-again believers; we were not even particularly religious; however, something very special—even sacred—had been passed down for generations in our Catholic, French-Canadian family.

This New Year's blessing imparted something of lasting value to me. Just a few days ago my mother and I discussed this practice and she told me that, as a child, she also received a yearly blessing from her father. Maybe this is one key to her incredible strength and positive view of life. I no longer have my father, for he recently passed into glory; however, I will always cherish my memories of him and the blessings he imparted to me.

JACOB CREATED A NEW FAMILY TRADITION

After all Jacob went through to get his father's blessing, it is interesting that, when the time had nearly come for Jacob to breathe his last, he didn't make an issue over the blessing being the birthright of his firstborn. Instead, he blessed all his sons and even Joseph's sons:

Genesis 48:5
"And now your two sons, Ephraim and Manasseh, who were born to you in the land of Egypt before I came to you in Egypt, are mine; as Reuben and Simeon, they shall be mine."

Genesis 48:20
So he blessed them that day, saying, "By you Israel will bless, saying, 'May God make you as Ephraim and as Manasseh!'" And thus he set Ephraim before Manasseh.

Not only did he bless; he prophesied over every one of them. Could it be that he realized the damage that had been done by the limited concept of blessing held by previous generations? Could it be that he realized he had not just one, but infinite blessings to bestow upon his children and grandchildren? I believe, in this way, we need to be like Jacob. Our ability to impart blessing is limitless. As God pours into us, we can pour into those who are members of our family, as well as those who are not.

I've noticed, through the years, that many adults grew up without a sense that they were blessed and cherished by their parents. Some parents have even been guilty of withholding love or acceptance, as a form of discipline. I'll never forget when I witnessed a young adult being disowned by an angry father. It made me so angry. There are much better ways to discipline our children. Later in this book, we will discuss them; however, can we all agree that we will be those who bless, love and give to our families? Can we ask our heavenly Father to help us and fill us with the ability to bless, without measure or prejudice?

Job also learned from his prior parental errors. After losing his first ten children to a terrible tragedy, he had ten more children. Although he always had concerns about his first ten children, something seemed to have shifted with his second set of ten children. Read this passage and see if you can discover the remarkable differences in his parenting style.

Job 42:15
In all the land were found no women so beautiful as the daughters of Job; and their father gave them an inheritance among their brothers.

Job makes a revolutionary decision to give his daughters equal shares of his financial legacy. Wow. That is completely amazing. He set an incredible precedence for future leaders who loved their children. In his culture, women did not receive shares in the inheritance. Job decided to bless all his children: not just the young men. Job realized that he had more to give to all his children. Job was a father who embraced his role and his new children with zealous dedication.

THE FATHERLESS GENERATION

Through observation and my studies in psychology, I have discovered a phenomenon that has recently been dubbed by the media as "the fatherless generation." I'm not sure who first made this observation or coined this term, but I do agree with it. Here are a few statistics that will make your head spin and prove that the lack of fathering has crippled our culture. My prayer is: "Oh, God, please turn the hearts of the fathers in America back to their children."

Divorce Rate Statistics in America

According to DivorceRate.org:

41% of first marriages fail.
60% of second marriages fail.
73% of third marriages fail.

With such a high rate of divorce, many parents are faced to raise their children alone. Unfortunately, that full burden often lands on the wife. Here are a few frightening statistics:

Fatherless Homes Statistics

According to FatherMag.com, children of fatherless homes are:

- Five times more likely to commit suicide.
- Thirty two times more likely to runaway.
- Fourteen times more likely to commit rape.
- Nine times more likely to drop out of high school.
- Twenty times more likely to end up in prison.
- Ten times more likely to abuse chemical substances.

If you are a single parent, do not be alarmed, but be informed. Single parents can raise incredible children if they align themselves with God (who is a father to the fatherless), as well as other key leaders in their church and community.

My friend Mike Gottfried (the famous ESPN announcer) started an incredible ministry called "Team Focus". Its primary focus is to provide surrogate fathers to hurting, fatherless boys. Each leader in his ministry helps transform the kids, by providing four primary resources: **attention, affection, affirmation and authority**. Isn't that a recipe for success? Every son or daughter needs that. In a recent USA Today article, it was mentioned that one in every one-hundred adults is incarcerated. If you were to interview the inmates, I imagine that most of them did not have a significant father figure in their lives. Why has violence skyrocketed among youth in the past ten years? Could it be that the fathers are AWOL, due to drugs, crime, ambition, pornography or addictions?

In Las Vegas we recently had three school shootings in one week. Fear is gripping our middle school and high school campuses. None of us will also forget the Virginia Tech massacre and the recent shooting at the University of Illinois. Could the divorce rate in America contribute to the rise of violent crime? I believe that there are a few more contributing factors to the emergence of the fatherless generation:

- Single-parent families have a more difficult time juggling a career, bills and parenting. How many single-parent homes are in your church or community? Who is helping them through their struggles?
- Studies have shown that up to one in four girls and one out of six boys is sexually abused by the age of eighteen. Abuse creates a growing populace that will struggle with self-esteem, anger, rage and depression.
- The violent movies, music and computer games seem to have desensitized a generation to violence and murder. Could the old saying, "garbage in; garbage out" be true?
- The Bible and religion have officially been removed from the public school system. If you take God out of schools, what do you have left? A godless society. Although we know that God will truly never be taken out of schools (there are far too many on fire teachers and students for this to happen) the policies that govern certain school systems have dishonored the God who helped America become great.

WHO'S IN CONTROL?

It is important, as we consider these facts, to ask ourselves what our roles are in the family. What can we do about these families that are in crisis? Here are the answers:

Joshua 24:15

"And if it seems evil to you to serve the LORD, choose for yourselves this day whom you will serve, whether the gods which your fathers served that were on the other side of the River, or the gods of the Amorites, in whose land you dwell. But as for me and my house, we will serve the LORD."

Joshua—the great leader of the Jewish nation—knew that he could not control everyone. He was sure that he could lead the multitudes, but deep down, he knew that God gave everyone the power to choose. Theologians call this "free will." It means that, since God created mankind in His image, all mankind would have the ability to make choices. Choices that could even violate His perfect will and mess up people's lives. Joshua made his role very clear: I am the head of my family; they will follow my lead in righteousness and serving God.

In Matthew, Jesus also made Himself very clear when He said, *"He who has ears to hear, let him hear!"* (Matthew 13:9). Jesus knew that free-will human-beings would either listen and change or miss it and be lost forever. He loved them all, but He knew they all had free will. For over 20 years I have taught people that they are responsible for their thoughts, feelings and actions. Everyone's role in life is to accept this responsibility and exercise their free will in ways that will glorify God. If they steward their thoughts, feelings and actions in a biblical way, they are not responsible for the thoughts, feelings and actions of others. James illustrates this principle, by underlining how difficult it is to even control our tongues:

James 3:8-10
But no man can tame the tongue. It is an unruly evil, full of deadly poison. With it we bless our God and Father, and with it we curse men, who have been made in the similitude of God. Out of the same mouth proceed blessing and cursing. My brethren, these things ought not to be so.

THE BIG THREE

Everyone is responsible for their own "big three." In other words: If you understand your role in family transformation and faithfully live it, you can't control how others will respond. They have their roles and responsibilities; you have yours. It is not easy to master your thoughts and feelings. I can guarantee you that it is even more difficult to accept the responsibility for the role of others. If you can faithfully accomplish your God-given role, you will be ale to sleep well at night, knowing that most people can't even control their tongues. Don't forget that your number-one goal is to fulfill your biblical role and pray for everyone else, so that they will have the same grace and strength from God to fulfill theirs. With the uprising of fatherless homes and violence, this question can be asked: "So, what is my role to help my family succeed?" So, let's talk a little bit about the different roles each one of us can play in the transformation of our families.

THE ROLE OF FATHERS

Dads, we have already spoken about the consequences of this fatherless generation. It is a clear and present danger that is threatening our society. Your role is biblically clear. So, let's live it out:

- **Love your wives.**

Ephesians 5:25
Husbands love your wives, just as Christ also loved the church and gave Himself for her . . .

- **Train and educate your children.**

Proverbs 22:6
Train up a child in the way he should go,
And when he is old he will not depart from it.

- **Support your family through hard work.**

1 Timothy 5:8
But if anyone does not provide for his own, and especially for those of his household, he has denied the faith and is worse than an unbeliever.

- **Discipline your children.**

Hebrews 12:7-8
If you endure chastening, God deals with you as with sons; for what son is there whom a father does not chasten? But if you are without chastening, of which all have become partakers, then you are illegitimate and not sons.

- **Be the spiritual priests of your home.**

1 Timothy 3:12
Let deacons be the husbands of one wife, ruling their children and their own houses well.

- **Be a faithful, godly man.**

2 Timothy 2:2
And the things that you have heard from me among many witnesses, commit these to faithful men who will be able to teach others also.

THE ROLE OF MOTHERS

- **Respect your husbands.**

Colossians 3:18
Wives, submit to your own husbands, as is fitting in the Lord.

- **Influence your husband by your speech and character.**

1 Peter 3:3-4
Do not let your adornment be merely outward—arranging the hair, wearing gold, or putting on fine apparel—rather let it be the hidden person of the heart, with the incorruptible beauty of a gentle and quiet spirit, which is very precious in the sight of God.

- **Establish a nurturing, well disciplined home.**

Proverbs 31:27
She watches over the ways of her household,
And does not eat the bread of idleness.

- **Be a spiritual force in your family.**

2 Timothy 1:5
. . . when I call to remembrance the genuine faith that is in you, which dwelt first in your grandmother Lois and your mother Eunice, and I am persuaded is in you also.

- **Be a force in your community, church and beyond.**

Proverbs 31:20
She extends her hand to the poor,
Yes, she reaches out her hands to the needy.

THE ROLE OF GRANDPARENTS

Although you are not the primary caregivers of your grandchildren, your role is still pivotal.

- **Your adult offspring still need you.**

Proverbs 5:1
My son, pay attention to my wisdom;
Lend your ear to my understanding . . .

- **You are an elder in your family.**

Titus 2:2-3
. . . that the older men be sober, reverent, temperate, sound in faith, in love, in patience; the older women likewise, that they be reverent in behavior, not slanderers, not given to much wine, teachers of good things...

- **You are a spiritual force for generations.**

Job 42:16
After this Job lived one hundred and forty years, and saw his children and grandchildren for four generations.

- **You are an intercessor for your clan.**

1 Thessalonians 5:16-18
Rejoice always, pray without ceasing, in everything give thanks; for this is the will of God in Christ Jesus for you.

- **You are a source of stability and wealth for your family.**

Job 42:12
Now the LORD blessed the latter days of Job more than his beginning; for he had fourteen thousand sheep, six thousand camels, one thousand yoke of oxen, and one thousand female donkeys.

- **You impart through your stories and experiences.**

Joel 1:3
Tell your children about it,
Let your children tell their children,
And their children another generation.

Baby-sit often. Pray without ceasing. Encourage them, help them, teach them and inspire them. Above all: Love them into their destinies.

The Role of Aunts and Uncles

Although, in most cases, you are not in the home of your cousins, brothers, sisters, nieces and nephews, you can still become a spiritual force and influence.

- **Give to them and help them as you are able.**

Isaiah 32:8
But a generous man devises generous things,
And by generosity he shall stand.

- **Pray for them.**

James 5:16
Confess your trespasses to one another, and pray for one another, that you may be healed. The effective, fervent prayer of a righteous man avails much.

- **Open up your home for them.**

1 Peter 4:9
Be hospitable to one another without grumbling.

- **Demonstrate the good news to them.**

1 Corinthians 2:4
And my speech and my preaching were not with persuasive words of human wisdom, but in demonstration of the Spirit and of power . . .

- **Share your testimony when they are open.**

Colossians 4:6
Let your speech always be with grace, seasoned with salt, that you may know how you ought to answer each one.

- **Minister to them when they are hurting.**

Colossians 3:12
Therefore, as the elect of God, holy and beloved, put on tender mercies, kindness, humility, meekness, longsuffering . . .

THE ROLE OF YOUNG ADULTS & TEENS

It may seem like you don't fit into a transformation plan for your family, but you do.

- **Honor your father and mother.**

Exodus 20:12
"Honor your father and your mother, that your days may be long upon the land which the LORD your God is giving you."

- **Forgive them when they fail you.**

2 Corinthians 2:10-11
Now whom you forgive anything, I also forgive. For if indeed I have forgiven anything, I have forgiven that one for your sakes in the presence of Christ, lest Satan should take advantage of us; for we are not ignorant of his devices.

- **Ask for forgiveness when you fail.**

Colossians 3:13
. . . bearing with one another, and forgiving one another, if anyone has a complaint against another; even as Christ forgave you, so you also must do.

- **Be willing to serve your parent.**

1 Kings 19:21
So Elisha turned back from him, and took a yoke of oxen and slaughtered them and boiled their flesh, using the oxen's equipment, and gave it to the people, and they ate. Then he arose and followed Elijah, and became his servant.

- **Be on fire for God.**

2 Timothy 1:6 (NIV)
For this reason I remind you to fan into flame the gift of God, which is in you through the laying on of my hands.

Young people, John Maxwell's book *The 360 Degree Leader* is a real winner. It is a perfect road map to help you lead from the position that you are in now.

OUR ROLES ARE CLEAR

As you think and pray about your role, ask God for wisdom. Be sure that you do not become co-dependant with family members. Each person will have to give account for their lives one day.

Romans 14:12
So then each of us shall give account of himself to God.

Ask God to help you faithfully administer and steward the gifts He has given you. Remember that, although you cannot control people, make them change or make them happy, you have the power to bless, love, influence, comfort, train and equip. Make sure that you are a giver and be a sower. Only God knows what seed will reap a harvest.

Be clear about your role and the role of others. Pray that every family member will experience the presence and power of the Holy Spirit. Pray that they will all grow into mature adults, find freedom and find purpose in their God-given roles. Never be afraid to sit with family members to clarify roles and responsibilities. The boundaries and levels of responsibility can often become blurred. Every marriage will need these discussions. Expectations and frustrations often emerge when roles are not clear. Once a couple clarifies the roles of every family member, life becomes easier.

I remember when my dad disagreed with a discipline method that Denise and I were using. Because Denise and I were on the same page, it gave me strength to respectfully tell my dad that, in our home, we would discipline in a biblical fashion. At first it was hard for him to swallow, but in time he accepted and appreciated the way we raised our children. Genesis 2 gives a practical example of family boundaries and roles.

Genesis 2:24
Therefore a man shall leave his father and mother and be joined to his wife, and they shall become one flesh.

That was not the only time that our unity as a couple was tested. Whether it was our kids testing the limits and our united front or a relationship from church that would try to steal our family life, we have often been challenged in this area. Roles, boundaries and expectations are still a big part of our family values.

Questions to Make You Think

Q: Did your parents freely give blessings to you and your siblings?

Q: Do you know your role? Is there any confusion with roles in your family?

CHAPTER 6

BREAKING OUT OF CYCLES AND CURSES

My mentor Dr. Richard Dobbins taught me a saying that I have used for over twenty four years: *"Until the pain of remaining the same is greater than the pain of change, people will stay the same."* In other words: People won't change until they are in enough pain. Most people don't like to change; they will avoid it as long as they can. It's scary, intimidating and painful. How much pain are you in right now? Is it enough to motivate you to break cycles that may be traced back three or four generations? If you want to turn your kids or grandkids around, or if you want to break generational curses, you will have to want it really bad! I'm convinced that, with Gods help, it is likely that you will become an agent of change for your whole family.

ISRAEL BROKE A NEGATIVE CYCLE

The ancient Israelites are a wonderful example of people who broke a very negative cycle of failure and bondage. Here is how they went about breaking the cycle in their nation:

1. They recognized their sin.

They recognized that sin—their own and that of past generations—had led to the terrible hardship and distress, in which they found themselves. They knew that deliverance, change and liberation could come only if they first humbled themselves, confessing and repenting of their sins and the sins of their fathers:

Nehemiah 9:1-3
Now on the twenty-fourth day of this month the children of Israel were assembled with fasting, in sackcloth, and with dust on their heads. Then those of Israelite lineage separated themselves from all foreigners; and they stood and confessed their sins and the iniquities of their fathers. And they stood up in their place and read from the Book of the Law of the LORD their God for one-fourth of the day; and for another fourth they confessed and worshiped the LORD their God.

2. They admitted their sin.

Can you imagine how it felt to admit their sins and the sins of their parents in front of all their friends and relatives? Remember that it was a public gathering. In order for Nehemiah and his followers to break the cycle of generational sins and their fallout, he had to lead them in public confession.

3. They confessed their sin.

Admitting the truth may hurt, but it sets us free. It also defeats any ugly pride that may be lurking in the shadows. Pride cannot survive when exposed to the light of confession and repentance. About 500 years after Nehemiah jotted down his memoirs, the writings of the apostle James expressed his belief that confession to other believers was still a good, healthy practice.

James 5:16
Confess your trespasses to one another, and pray for one another, that you may be healed. The effective, fervent prayer of a righteous man avails much.

An open family who is able to discuss their weaknesses with each other, confess their sins and provide opportunities for reconciliation will be a healthier family. When was the last time you asked your family for forgiveness? When was the last time you admitted error, weakness or sin? What would happen if you started today?

Recognizing our weaknesses and sins, admitting them to our families and confessing them to God are three important ingredients in creating a movement out of a negative cycle. Recognizing requires true insight and honesty, which means no more denial. Admitting requires opens discussion as a family or with your friends. Confession requires humility and integrity.

4. They recognized their need for repentance.

The fourth ingredient that facilitates a breakthrough is repentance. Repentance means that one is sorry for what he or she has done. It means that the person wants to think differently and change the way that he or she behaves. It requires statements such as: "I am sorry; please forgive me. I know that my actions or words must have hurt you; please forgive me. What can I do to make it up to you? I am committed to ceasing that behavior and I will do whatever I need to do to get the help I need to change. I love you."

Cycles can be broken by dedicated people. I've seen countless men, women and teens who have changed dramatically. In most cases their dramatic changes create a change movement in their families.

FREEDOM FROM OUR PAST

2 Corinthians 5:17
Therefore, if anyone is in Christ, he is a new creation; old things have passed away; behold, all things have become new.

Through sixteen years of leading our church and training parents, I have discovered that a common thread that troubles a family is their battle to break free from their past. Many parents and couples have complained to me that they struggle with memories and weaknesses from their parents. Some of their challenges can even be traced back to several generations. We call these struggles "generational problems" or "generational curses." Let's unwrap this concept a little further and discover how to break generational curses.

BREAKING GENERATIONAL CURSES

Before our children can verbalize, they learn by observation. The images they observe are connected to feelings and sensations. Those connections are the most powerful influences on personality and emotional health; they are the most difficult to change, because they are pre-verbal. Even when they learn to speak, young children do not have the sophistication to process negative experiences in healthy ways. Imagine the lasting effects on a child, when he or she grows up in a home where alcoholism, abuse, neglect, uncontrolled anger or manipulation has always been part of the picture.

Perhaps you know, firsthand, what it's like for a child to go through one or more of these painful experiences. What kind of impartation did you receive by example? What did that seed develop in you and what fruit did it bear? Do you have the same spirit your mom and dad had? Do you have the same fears and struggles? It is not a coincidence. When the Bible tells us that *"a man reaps what he sows"* (Galatians 6:7), it is not referring only to what will be produced in his own life; it also includes the harvest that will result from what a parent sows into his or her child. Have you ever wondered why the sins of the father are transferred from generation to generation? Don't look any further. What perpetuates sin and its consequences is generational disobedience.

Exodus 20:5-6

". . . you shall not bow down to them nor serve them. For I, the LORD your God, am a jealous God, visiting the iniquity of the fathers upon the children to the third and fourth generations of those who hate Me, but showing mercy to thousands, to those who love Me and keep My commandments."

God's judgment is very real and His justice is perfect. Thankfully, His mercy is just as real, and His grace is freely given to all who come to Him with contrite and humble hearts. Someone recently asked me if it is possible to break the impact of the Exodus warning. The answer is a clear "yes." Breaking generational curses— or even God's judgment—is not easy, but the following steps will indeed provide the answers to see breakthrough in your life.

HOW TO BREAK GENERATIONAL CURSES:

A. Repent and ask God to forgive your father's sin and your personal sin. Every great revivalist of the Old Testament started by repenting for historical and generational sin.

Nehemiah 1:6

. . . please let Your ear be attentive and Your eyes open, that You may hear the prayer of Your servant which I pray before You now, day and

night, for the children of Israel Your servants, and confess the sins of the children of Israel which we have sinned against You. Both my father's house and I have sinned.

B. Ask God to cleanse you of any sins that you are not fully aware of. Ask for His mercy and grace to fill your life and family.

Psalm 139:23-24
Search me, O God, and know my heart;
Try me, and know my anxieties;
And see if there is any wicked way in me,
And lead me in the way everlasting.

C. Begin to honor your parents and mate in front of your children. If you have failed to do this in the past, God can forgive and help you.

D. Make a conscious choice to change behaviors. While I was growing up I made a conscious decision: "I want to be like that when I'm a dad." It's amazing how this helps me to attempt new behaviors and get the coaching I need.

Questions to Make You Think

Q: Are there family cycles that you want to shatter? What are they?

Q: Are there personal cycles that need to be broken? What are they?

Q: How will you break these old cycles?

Q: How do you feel about the example that you have been setting for your children?

Q: Are there any behaviors or attitudes that you would not encourage your children to emulate?

Q: What will you do to change these behaviors or attitudes?

CHAPTER 7

TRANSFORMATION IN OUR HOME

When Denise and I moved our family from Sacramento, California to Las Vegas, Nevada, to pastor a small, home missions church, our eldest daughter Isabelle—who was 11 at the time—reacted to the change very poorly. It crushed us to see our beloved little girl begin to make horrible decisions. There were several factors that led to her rebellion, but the enemy consistently tried to point the finger of guilt at Denise and I. He also tried to fill us with fear for her future.

We did everything we could to bring her back and we held on to every promise in the Word. We discovered new realms of spiritual warfare and learned how to pray under difficult circumstances. We evaluated our relationship and concluded that, although we are not a perfect family, we are a good family. The circumstances were our daughter's choice. For a season, she decided to step out from under the protective covering of our authority and walk away from our love.

Even though this season brought tremendous hurt, anger and grief, we did not allow the enemy of our souls to destroy our confidence in God, nor did we allow our daughter's bad decisions to destroy us as a family. Please do not forget that there is a supernatural battle being waged for our children. God loves them and has a plan for their lives, but Satan also has plans for them. He wants to kill them and use them to crush your faith and confidence in God. Don't allow Satan to carry out his plans. It's time to fight back.

It is common for parents to accept the blame when a child goes astray, but Denise and I refused to blame each other or ourselves. Playing the blame game is never constructive. If you find yourself dealing with a rebellious child, please do not allow Satan to pour the vinegar of guilt and shame into your wounds. Don't forget that Satan is the accuser of the brethren (Revelation 12:10) and that he is a liar; there is no truth in him (John 8:44).

Our experience with rebellion in our family has driven home the great impact we make in our role as parents, but it has also made us more aware than ever of our utter-dependence on God. I am pleased to say that, a decade later, Isabelle is now serving God with her whole heart. She feels that she is called to have a ministry and has committed her life to reaching out to hurting people. Our daughter's battle with cancer has only served to solidify her desire to serve the Lord.

Not only has Isabelle been physically healed; she has blossomed into a wonderful woman of God, as a wife and mother. The joy that Denise and I now have, as we watch her interact with her wonderful husband and incredible son is almost beyond expression. Even as I am writing these notes, I'm fighting back tears. God is so good. Many times, Denise and I quoted this verse:

Proverbs 22:6
Train up a child in the way he should go,
And when he is old he will not depart from it.

Our wonderful Isabelle has just finished her Master's degree in psychology, just like her dad. There is no doubt in my mind that the double-portion blessing is on her life. Denise and I have claimed this verse for every area of our lives. We have contended for our children's destinies with the Word, fasting, prayer and the power of agreement.

DOUBLE PORTION

Joel 2:23-25
Be glad then, you children of Zion,
And rejoice in the LORD your God;
For He has given you the former rain faithfully, And He will cause the rain to come down for you—
The former rain,
And the latter rain in the first month.
The threshing floors shall be full of wheat,
And the vats shall overflow with new wine and oil.
"So I will restore to you the years that the swarming locust has eaten,
The crawling locust,
The consuming locust,
And the chewing locust, My great army which I sent among you."

Notice that it mentions that God will send the former and latter rain in the same month. That's a double portion for all the parents and children who have gone through a difficult season. It is double portion time!

For those of you who are facing the same type of trials, please know that, with God's help, you will make it. Let's decree together that all the wayward sons and daughters will return to God, better than ever. Shout it out and believe it! The Bible promises that, if you will declare it, He will establish it. Decree that your children will serve God; be successful; find the perfect mate and be used by the Holy Spirit. God will establish it!

Denise and I have learned many important lessons through these trials. In the pages that follow, I would like to share some of what we have discovered. If you put these ideas into practice, you can't help but become a more effective parent and a more powerful imparter. Your children will also reach their full potential in Jesus Christ.

REAL TRANSFORMATION

Real transformation begins with a spiritual focus. The first commandment that God gave to Moses was spiritual in nature:

Deuteronomy 6:5
You shall love the LORD your God with all your heart, with all your soul, and with all your strength.

Getting our bodies, minds and spirits in line with our Creator is the most important, first step toward transformation. Jesus taught His followers the priority sequence:

Matthew 22:37-39
Jesus said to him, "'You shall love the LORD your God with all your heart, with all your soul, and with all your mind.' This is the first and great commandment. And the second is like it: 'You shall love your neighbor as yourself.'"

Real transformation, in its deepest sense, must start with our spiritual lives. Transformation is generally started by an impartation of knowledge, wisdom, revelation, anointing, forgiveness, love or spirit. In 2 Kings, Elisha saw the life of his mentor Elijah as something to be emulated. Since Elisha wanted to follow in Elijah's footsteps, he did not ask for a chariot, home or pasture. Elisha asked for a double portion of Elijah's spirit.

2 Kings 2:9
And so it was, when they had crossed over, that Elijah said to Elisha, "Ask! What may I do for you, before I am taken away from you?" Elisha said, "Please let a double portion of your spirit be upon me."

As parents, we have all made mistakes and we will make a few more before heaven greets us. However, the number-one ingredient that will either repel or attract our children to our beliefs is our spirit. Every human-being has their own spirit. It is that immeasurable, God-given center that has the potential to reflect God. When we were created in His image, we weren't designed to look like Him, physically, but to *be* like Him. God is spirit; we were created with a body, soul and spirit to represent Him.

BE FULL OF HIS SPIRIT

When our spirits are full of His Spirit, we reflect the glory of God. We release the gifts and fruits of the Holy Spirit all around. Your children will want to be around you, because you pour out love, joy, peace, patience and kindness. Your children will be drawn to parents who have spirits that are full of God's Spirit. They will want a double portion and they will want to follow in our footsteps. When you go to the ice-cream parlor, do you order a single scoop or a double scoop? You will probably order only a single scoop, unless, of course, you really love the flavor. Your children will live out this same principle, as they relate to you. They will either grow up saying, "I never want to be like them" or, "Wow, I love and respect them. I want to be just like them."

OPTIONS

Just over a year ago, my son Samuel was in his final year of high-school: a good student and athlete, surrounded by friends, temptations and all that the world has to offer. I sat with him one afternoon and laid it all out on the table. I said, "Son, if you follow the world's standards and live for yourself, I can't help you very much. Someone is going to get a double portion of my spirit, I hope and pray that it will be you, but you have to make that choice." No one can force your children to be godly, loving, productive, giving or kind. They have to choose this often. It has to appear attractive to them: not just a bunch of rules, but a vibrant, good-news type of belief system.

Is your faith positive, uplifting and fun? Does it cause your attitude to be amazing? Is the atmosphere in your home warm and inviting? I hope so, because a home like this will attract your children and their friends to accept Christ.

My son Samuel clearly saw his two options: Live for God and get in position to receive a double portion of the spirit that fills my dad or follow the world. Samuel chose to follow God and his dad. A few months later he was stricken with a horrible, neurological disease. I am convinced that Satan wanted to steal, kill and destroy our son. Satan wanted to snatch the seed while it was new. Praise God that our son was powerfully healed by Jesus Christ. My wife and I leaned heavily on Genesis 50:20 during Isabelle's bout with cancer and Samuel's bout with Guillain-Barré.

Genesis 50:20

"But as for you, you meant evil against me; but God meant it for good, in order to bring it about as it is this day, to save many people alive."

From our trials came amazing results:

1. Samuel was healed. He learned about prayer, nutrition and physical health. (For more information, see: *Perfect Health: The Natural Way* by Mary-Ann Shearer). Our whole family has grown through these lessons.

2. We became very connected with Lou and Therese Engle: two amazing world-changers. Lou and his assistant, Thomas, fasted over two weeks for Samuel's healing. Lou also laid hands on our son to receive a Nazarite anointing. I can testify that he did receive it. Our son received a call to follow in my footsteps. He has committed himself, one-hundred percent, to live for God. He has also felt called to start our house of prayer at our church: the International Church of Las Vegas. It's so inspiring to see a 19-year-old demonstrate this level of dedication. Some of you may have seen Isabelle's healing testimony on Christian television or read about it in one of my books. Her story truly did reach hundreds of thousands. What the enemy meant for harm, God used for the good: the saving of many souls.

THE HOLY SPIRIT AT THE CENTER

If you place the Holy Spirit first in your life, parenting becomes a much easier venture. Don't get me wrong; allowing the Holy Spirit of Christ to lead and guide me is still a struggle. It's a daily decision to let "Jesus take the wheel." One of the products of a Holy-Spirit life is the impact it has on our children. All three of my children love God and serve Him. They admire and respect their parents and serve at the church, while pursuing their callings. Isabelle is dedicated to Christian counseling and wellness centers. Christine leads in prayer and the prophetic song. Samuel is starting the house of prayer. The journey has not been easy, but God has adopted my children and they have embraced Him. I've always tried to put God first in my life, my wife second, my kids third and ministry forth. Denise and I have tried to live a Spirit-filled and Spirit-led life. We've committed to seeking and serving God with all our hearts.

YOUR FAMILY DNA

Every family will develop its own personality and set of spoken and unspoken rules. These priorities become the foundation of the family. They help set the atmosphere and create an environment for creativity, love, excellence, hospitality or the opposite. I call these cornerstone characteristics "the family DNA." I've listed a few of the key elements of our family DNA. I hope they will help you. After you've read ours, please take a few moments and write down what your family DNA looks like. If you can't figure it out, ask friends and family to help you determine what your family is all about. Family DNA is pretty difficult to hide. Find a few people who can be blunt and honest with you. We've concluded that, if we kept the following priorities in the forefront, our kids will follow. Here are some of the things that we have established in our home:

- Be real. No one likes fake people. Be honest about your struggles, feelings and set backs.
- Be positive. Lead with a vision for your home, family and finances. Joshua said, *"But as for me and my house, we will serve the Lord"* (Joshua 24:15).
- Be forgiving. I've practiced this a thousand times, because I live by the principle: *"Do not let the sun go down on your wrath . . ."* (Ephesians 4:26).
- Be loving. Express love verbally and physically, every day.
- Be an encourager. Life will be tough. So, keep encouraging your children daily.
- Be a role model for marriage. If you are married, invest in this relationship by having weekly date nights, showing lots

of affection and saying positive words. If you are a single parent, help your children find positive role models in the extended family or at church.

- Be consistent. Consistency is so important to help your children feel secure and confident. Church attendance and daily, healthy habits are crucial.
- Be full of the Spirit. Our faith has to be intact and living, in order to pour out lasting gems to our children.
- Resolve conflict quickly.
- Don't compare yourself to others. Be the best you can be and leave the rest up to God.

Perhaps you've come to the conclusion that you need to experience a spiritual breakthrough. Can we agree, in prayer, for our homes and our children?

DEAR LORD JESUS, I DEDICATED MY CHILDREN TO YOU WHEN THEY WERE YOUNG SO TODAY I WANT TO AFFIRM MY DECISION. I GIVE YOU MY CHILDREN AGAIN. I ASK THAT YOU WILL TOUCH AND TRANSFORM THEM. HELP ME BECOME THE PARENT YOU'VE CALLED ME TO BE AND HELP THEM REACH THEIR DIVINE POTENTIAL. I ASK THIS IN JESUS' NAME.

_____

_____

Questions to Make You Think

- What is your family DNA?

- What would you like it to look like in 6 months from today?

CHAPTER 8

THE ROLE OF DISCIPLINE

iscipline is an important element of impartation that will help
you transfer principles, habits and attitudes to your children.
There are a few important truths about family discipline that Denise and I have learned and practiced through the past twenty-seven
years that I would like to share with you.

1. Discipline is different than punishment. All forms of discipline
   should be a vehicle for education, instead of an act of anger, or
   consequences for disobedience. Whether you spank a young
   child, send them to a corner or call a time out, remember that
   your child is learning something important. Ask yourself,
   "What are they learning?"

2. Discipline should never be done in anger. Parents should never
   strike out at a child or take out their anger on them. Discipline
   should be administered in a calm fashion. If you need a time-
   out before you administer the discipline, please take the time to
   cool down. It is easier to say, "Wait for me in your room" or,
   "Sit on that chair for a moment, until I return," than to pick up
   the pieces of discipline done in anger.

James 1:20

. . . for the wrath of man does not produce the righteousness of God.

Your anger will not make your child more godly or better be-
haved. It will not produce the righteousness of God. Therefore,
learn to control and process anger issues, so that they will not nega-
tively affect your home. If you have failed in this area, it is appropri-
ate to ask for forgiveness from God and from your child, then seek
help to overcome anger motivated discipline.

3. The strategies of discipline are important to decide upon before
   you have children. Here are a few reminders as you review your
   discipline options:

   - The more you can use logical consequences of behaviors, the
     more real and relevant it becomes to a child. In other words:
     Try to find the most logical consequences to disobedience.
     For example: If a child constantly fails to finish a paper, in-
     stead of rescuing them at the last minute, help your child
     connect the dots. As parents, we want to help them learn
     that certain behaviors or habits bring pain and others bring
     pleasure. Logical consequences of not preparing a paper
     could mean a "D" or an "F" grade. A "D" or an "F" brings
     negative consequences: more chores, less computer time or
     less TV. An "A" or a "B" grade, on the other hand, gives the
     child rewards and privileges.

   - Create a strong and clear reward system for the positive be-
     haviors that you want your children to adopt. Rewards can
     also be offered to encourage character traits, such as honesty,
     kindness, a positive attitude and so many other attributes
     that are important. Discipline does not only involve forms
     of negative deterrents, but positive reinforcements as well. In
     other words: Create a constant reward system for desired be-

havior and consequences that are negative for undesirable behaviors.

4. Make sure that both parents are on the same page, in regard to strategy and methods of discipline. Consistency, fairness and clarity are so crucial to a child. Their self-esteem and character will be built on a firm foundation of rules, expectations, clear communication and consequences. Being a unified team, in regard to child-rearing, is a priority. Even if the parents are divorced, parenting is still something that will have to be accomplished together. If only one parent is involved in discipline, it will be more difficult to be successful; however, with God, all things are possible.

5. Single parents can be very successful parents, with the grace of God and help from strategic friends and family. Single parents can find allies in the parenting journey, through pastors, coaches, teachers, church leaders and other resources. If you are a single parent, God also promises that He will be a father to the fatherless (Psalm 68:5). I believe that God will help you team up with important resources and people to help your child become a world-changer. Team Focus is a wonderful resource and it is coming to a city near you. (For more information, please visit: www.teamfocusonline.org)

6. Do not forget that discipline must be nurtured by the desire to develop character and discipline in a child's life. We are all trying to raise mature, God-loving, successful adults. Everything we do in discipline is to prepare our children for the world we live in. In other words: We are a launching pad for our kids.

7. Never forget that love has to be the force that directs all of our discipline strategies and methods.

Proverbs 10:12
Hatred stirs up strife,
But love covers all sins.

All of us will make our share of parenting blunders; however, the power of unconditional love will be strong enough to make up for them all. **True love is unconditional.** We must love our children with the same love that Christ loves us. God's parenting approach with us is complete love. Let's ask the Holy Spirit of God to empower us to love our children unconditionally.

CHAPTER 9

TRANSFORMATIONAL KEYS

There are several keys that God has given us to build a spiritually-healthy family. As you apply these keys, you will set your family on the road to recovery and acceleration. Isn't this what God really wants for you? Don't settle for anything less. Isaiah 44:3 gives us powerful promises that should motivate us to go for all that God has for us:

Isaiah 44:3
"For I will pour water on him who is thirsty,
And floods on the dry ground;
I will pour My Spirit on your descendants,
And My blessing on your offspring . . ."

"I will pour My Spirit out on your descendants." That's what we pray for. That's what we need more than ever. We have this Scripture engraved on the side of our main sanctuary. We live in Las Vegas, which is a wasteland of broken lives for many, but for others it is an oasis of God's presence. The Bible promised that, *"Where sin abounded, grace abounded much more"* (Romans 5:20). Even though

we have lived in Las Vegas for 16 years, we have seen the grace of God touch and transform our family. We've discovered that the following keys will release transformation in your life.

TRANSFORMATION KEY 1: UNDERSTAND GOD'S PLAN

In 2 Corinthians, the apostle Paul reveals God's ultimate plan for our lives and families.

2 Corinthians 3:18
But we all, with unveiled face, beholding as in a mirror the glory of the Lord, are being transformed into the same image from glory to glory, just as by the Spirit of the Lord.

God wants to lead us to ever-increasing glory. Can you believe this? God has a great plan for you and your family. If this is truly God's will for you, then what is stopping you from tapping into these plans of good, progress and blessing? Have you ever battled with generational curses, ignorance, dead traditions, addictions, prejudices and other societal or cultural strongholds? God's intention for your family is to set it on a new journey of glory.

More Blessings

Jeremiah 29:11-13
For I know the thoughts that I think toward you, says the Lord, thoughts of peace and not of evil, to give you a future and a hope. Then you will call upon Me and go and pray to Me, and I will listen to you. And you will seek Me and find Me, when you search for Me with all your heart.

God wants to bless you and your family. He wants to help you fulfill your ultimate destiny. He is willing to fill you with His power (For more information on *The 5 Powers of God*, visit: www.iclv.com), gifts, talents and wisdom to chart a new course for your family. Notice that Jeremiah 29:11 tells us, when we believe that He has a great plan for us, we will seek Him in a new, passionate way. I truly believe that many Christians do not call, seek or search, because their view of God is distorted.

Our View of God

In 1986 God gave me a series of workbooks that unveiled the problem of our "God-concepts." (For more information on the *The Breakthrough Series*, visit: www.iclv.com) A God concept is the way we see and feel about God. Dr. Dobbins once said that our self-concepts are largely formed by three years of age, while our God-concept is formed by age five. The formulating years of our lives create the foundation for how we each view ourselves, others and God. These views are highly resistant to change.

Romans 8:7
Because the carnal mind is enmity against God; for it is not subject to the law of God, nor indeed can be.

Your ideas and feelings about God will form the foundation for your family for generations. Although our self-concepts and God-concepts are resistant to change, the Word of God declares that it is possible and necessary. This type of revelation can set you on your next journey. This is God's will for you and your family.

1 Corinthians 2:16
For "who has known the mind of the LORD that he may instruct Him?" But we have the mind of Christ.

Romans 12:1-2
I beseech you therefore, brethren, by the mercies of God, that you present your bodies a living sacrifice, holy, acceptable to God, which is your

reasonable service. And do not be conformed to this world, but be transformed by the renewing of your mind, that you may prove what is that good and acceptable and perfect will of God.

Ephesians 4:23-24

. . . and be renewed in the spirit of your mind, and that you put on the new man which was created according to God, in true righteousness and holiness.

TRANSFORMATION KEY 2:
DISCOVER THE STAGES OF PROGRESS

In the following illustration, you will see what I have called the "Circle of Progress". Someone once said that life is circular. I believe that this is true. Like the nation of Israel, many of us go around the same desert for years, until we experience a breakthrough of insight, leadership, revelation or God's power. Israel spent 40 years in the desert. They spent 40 years in the land of "coulda, woulda and shoulda."

Breakthroughs can be traced upon the Circle of Progress. Breakthrough is not a matter of luck or wishful thinking. It can be observed, analyzed and repeated. Let's take a moment to review the stages of progress, so that you will be able to chart and lead your family into the promised land.

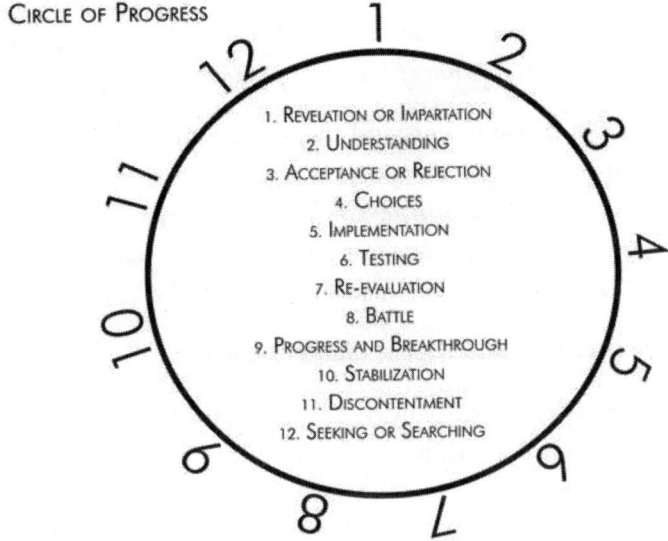

CIRCLE OF PROGRESS

1. REVELATION OR IMPARTATION
2. UNDERSTANDING
3. ACCEPTANCE OR REJECTION
4. CHOICES
5. IMPLEMENTATION
6. TESTING
7. RE-EVALUATION
8. BATTLE
9. PROGRESS AND BREAKTHROUGH
10. STABILIZATION
11. DISCONTENTMENT
12. SEEKING OR SEARCHING

Stage One: Revelation is what sparks a new cycle of progress. It can come directly from God, through a great teaching or insight from a counselor. Impartation can also cause a series of changes or repercussions. God can send you gifts or power that will serve as seeds of transformation.

- *Pray that God will fill your children with revelation and impartation.*

Stage Two: Every revelation can be understood or misunderstood. Jesus gave many revelations in His teachings, but still said, *"If anyone has ears to hear, let him hear!"* (Mark 7:16). In other words: "I know that all of you are not going to get this, but some of you will. So, here it goes!!!" Revelation and impartations are seeds that can develop into great harvests, or they can be wasted.

- *Pray that your children will understand what God is doing.*

John 12:24

"Most assuredly, I say to you, unless a grain of wheat falls into the ground and dies, it remains alone; but if it dies, it produces much grain."

Stage Three: Once you understand the revelation, the battle of accepting or not accepting it is important and real. 1 Corinthians 13:12 says, *"For now we see in a mirror, dimly, but then face to face."* Jeremiah declared, *"The heart is deceitful above all things, and desperately wicked; who can know it?"* (Jeremiah 17:9).

- *Pray that they will accept God's deposit.*

Stage Four: Revelation will always be followed by a series of options and choices that are different and challenging.

Isaiah 1:18
"Come now, and let us reason together,"
Says the LORD,
"Though your sins are like scarlet,
They shall be as white as snow;
Though they are red like crimson,
They shall be as wool."

- *Pray that they will make the right choices.*

Stage Five: Implementing good choices is always very difficult. Whether it's quitting coffee or working out, it is a challenge to change our lifestyles or our spiritual levels.

Joshua 24:15
And if it seems evil to you to serve the LORD, choose for yourselves this day whom you will serve, whether the gods which your fathers served that were on the other side of the River, or the gods of the Amorites, in whose land you dwell. But as for me and my house, we will serve the LORD.

- *Pray that they have wisdom to implement the changes.*

Stage Six: Testing. Healthy decisions will always be tested by the family and societal systems that surround you. You will face resistance to change.

James 1:3-4

. . . knowing that the testing of your faith produces patience. But let patience have its perfect work, that you may be perfect and complete, lacking nothing.

Deuteronomy 13:1-3

"If there arises among you a prophet or a dreamer of dreams, and he gives you a sign or a wonder, and the sign or the wonder comes to pass, of which he spoke to you, saying, 'Let us go after other gods'—which you have not known—'and let us serve them,' you shall not listen to the words of that prophet or that dreamer of dreams, for the LORD your God is testing you to know whether you love the LORD your God with all your heart and with all your soul."

- ***Pray that they will stand firm during the trials and tests.***

Stage Seven: Re-evaluation. After choices are tested, it is common for people to review whether the changes were worth the resistance. The price tag attached to all change can be quite overwhelming. In many cases, people question whether the changes are worth the pain, or they question whether they really heard God's directives clearly.

Joshua 1:2-3

"Moses My servant is dead. Now therefore, arise, go over this Jordan, you and all this people, to the land which I am giving to them—the children of Israel. Every place that the sole of your foot will tread upon I have given you, as I said to Moses."

<u>Numbers 13:33</u>
"There we saw the giants (the descendants of Anak came from the giants); and we were like grasshoppers in our own sight, and so we were in their sight."

- **Pray that they will be willing to sacrifice for progress.**

Stage Eight: If you decide that you want to keep moving toward new levels of glory, get ready to go to battle. Winston Churchill—the greatest leader of England—was once faced with a horrible barrage of V1 and V2, launched by the Nazi army. The bombs pounded military and civilian targets in London and other key sites. Churchill's radio response will never be forgotten by all of us who refuse to accept defeat: "I will never, never, never surrender."

At the threshold of every great breakthrough, there will be bloodshed. (For more information on *Crossing Your Next Threshold*, visit: www.iclv.com)

<u>Joshua 5:2-3</u>
At that time the LORD said to Joshua, "Make flint knives for yourself, and circumcise the sons of Israel again the second time." So Joshua made flint knives for himself, and circumcised the sons of Israel at the hill of the foreskins.

In our journey of progress, the blood that is shed is rarely human blood. Instead, it comes in the form of sacrifice, effort, hard work, faith, rejection or persecution. Are you ready for the battle that will gain you a great victory? Paul said, *"For we do not wrestle against flesh and blood, but against principalities, against powers, against the rulers of the darkness of this age, against spiritual hosts of wickedness in the heavenly places"* (Ephesians 6:12).

- **Pray that they will not give up the good fight of faith.**

Stage Nine: Victory is so sweet. After the battle comes progress and breakthrough. Paul said that we are more than conquerors:

Romans 8:37
Yet in all these things we are more than conquerors through Him who loved us.

New levels of joy, peace, happiness and success are reached during this stage. Celebrate your victories. Celebrate the milestones of progress. As a family learn to celebrate the victories of your children. Birthdays are big in our family. Anniversaries are so important! Graduations should be marked with rewards and recognition. Teach your family members to celebrate the individual accomplishments of their brothers, sisters, parents, cousins, aunts and uncles. Create a culture in which extra honor is given to all those who pay a price.

Reward victories; discipline disobedience and disrespect. Encourage those who are struggling. Get them the help they need to accomplish their dreams. Don't allow jealousy or sibling rivalry to seep into your home. Prioritize finding everyone's gifts and achievements, in order to celebrate their unique place in the family. Someone once said, "Praise in public and discipline in private." Denise and I have tried to follow this proverb, unless the child disobeyed in a public setting. When the violation is public, apologies are encouraged publicly.

- *Pray that your children will become overcomers.*

Stage Ten: Stabilization. After the new level is reached, it's important to possess new territory. Disciplines and strategies are important to keep the gains and not slip back to the old way of doing things. In World War II the allied forces had to secure the beaches of Anzio and Normandy, in order to fully deliver and possess the new territory.

Stage Eleven: Discontentment. After a period of time at the new level, discontentment is common. It's a sign that you are about to enter into a new circle of progress. It can manifest itself with a sense of spiritual hunger, frustration or dissatisfaction. Never forget that progress is only the next step of glory. We are not called to be fully satisfied at any level. We were designed by God to keep growing, creating and pressing.

Philippians 3:14
I press toward the goal for the prize of the upward call of God in Christ Jesus.

- **Pray that they find their way in this uncomfortable phase.**

Stage Twelve: Seeking or searching follows the hunger or discontentment. You will find new revelation and a new Circle of Progress will begin, because you will search for it. Many of us wonder why we were designed by God to keep going and fighting for more souls, progress and creativity. The answer is simple: We are created in God's image and God is a creative God; therefore, we are creative people. The only prayer that was taught by Jesus illustrates and confirms this mission:

Matthew 6:9-13
"In this manner, therefore, pray:
Our Father in heaven,
Hallowed be Your name.
Your kingdom come.
Your will be done
On earth as it is in heaven.
Give us this day our daily bread.
And forgive us our debts,
As we forgive our debtors.
And do not lead us into temptation,
But deliver us from the evil one.
For Yours is the kingdom and the power and the glory forever. Amen."

Our mission will only be done when we see His face.

- *Pray that they will seek and find God's voice during this time of transition.*

TRANSFORMATION KEY 3:
TAP INTO THE POWER OF PRAYER

James 5:16
Confess your trespasses to one another, and pray for one another, that you may be healed. The effective, fervent prayer of a righteous man avails much.

Prayer is a very dynamic and exciting means of transformation. It takes us out of the natural realm of child-rearing into the supernatural. Therefore, it has great potential to affect sudden, dramatic and miraculous changes in our children. In order to make sure you are ready to pray with power, you will have to take one more step of self-examination. You must ask yourself: "Do I believe that something actually happens when I pray?"

The Bible teaches us that, when we pray, we should expect the extraordinary, the supernatural and the miraculous. It says that we are to expect results that are *"exceedingly, abundantly above all that we ask or think"* (Ephesians 3:20). The Bible exhorts us to confess our sins to each other and pray for each other, so that we may be healed. It assures us that *"the prayer of a righteous man is powerful and effective"* (James 5:16 NIV). The Greek word used here for "powerful" is "ischuo" (is-khoo'-o), meaning "to have or exercise force (literally or figuratively)."

Power to Transform

Jesus taught us that our faith could move mountains.

Matthew 17:20
So Jesus said to them, "Because of your unbelief; for assuredly, I say to you, if you have faith as a mustard seed, you will say to this mountain, 'Move from here to there,' and it will move; and nothing will be impossible for you."

Why, then, wouldn't our prayers transform our children? I believe that most parents are too afraid to pray daring, extravagant prayers over their children. Filled with insecurity and self-doubt, they are satisfied with, "Now I lay me down to sleep..." We should be praying words like, "Dear God, fill my children with Your Holy Spirit. Give them a spirit of wisdom and discernment. Help them flee from youthful lust. Fill them with passionate love and insatiable hunger for You. Help them to walk in Your will for their lives and to fulfill the purpose, for which You created them."

Power to Impart

Deuteronomy 34:9
Now Joshua the son of Nun was full of the spirit of wisdom, for Moses had laid his hands on him; so the children of Israel heeded him, and did as the LORD had commanded Moses.

Joshua received wisdom through the prayer of his mentor. In other words: God took the spirit He had placed on Moses and gave it to Joshua. Wow! God can also take the same spirit that is in you and pour it into your children. Is that what you want for them? For example, would you want your children to have the same level of faith as you? If they did, would they (like Abel) be commended as righteous?

Hebrews 11:4
By faith Abel offered to God a more excellent sacrifice than Cain, through which he obtained witness that he was righteous, God testifying of his gifts; and through it he being dead still speaks.

Moms and dads, are you full of vibrant faith? Would God be pleased with your faith or would He rebuke you as Jesus did to some of His disciples?

Luke 12:28
"If then God so clothes the grass, which today is in the field and tomorrow is thrown into the oven, how much more will He clothe you, O you of little faith?"

If, after examining yourself, you find that you're lacking in faith, repent of your unbelief. Then, just as the father in the following passage of Scripture did, ask the Lord to help you in this area:

Mark 9:23-24
Jesus said to him, "If you can believe, all things are possible to him who believes." Immediately the father of the child cried out and said with tears, "Lord, I believe; help my unbelief!"

Step out and pray with the measure of faith you have been given. Remember: It only takes a mustard seed's worth. You will find the seed beginning to grow as you use it. Your prayers will pave the way for your children. Come into agreement with your mate, family or friends, for your children's mate selection, career, calling and friends.

TRANSFORMATION KEY 4: "THROUGH THE LAYING ON OF MY HANDS . . ."

Paul did not have any children of his own, but embraced Timothy as his son in the faith. Paul imparted spiritual gifts to Timothy, through his teachings, his example and the laying on of hands.

2 Timothy 1:6
Therefore I remind you to stir up the gift of God which is in you through the laying on of my hands.

Timothy received something real and observable. He had received a *charis,* which means: "a gift or divine gratuity". Why shouldn't our children be able to receive such gifts through us? If we can move a mountain with a prayer, can't we move the hearts of our children? Why wouldn't God use us to impart spiritual gifts to the next generation? When was the last time you laid your hands on your children, to pour out gifts, love, acceptance and affirmation?

Our experience with impartation prayer has played a huge role in the lives of all our children. At the church we pastor (the International Church of Las Vegas or ICLV), the pastoral staff and prayer team spend long periods of time at the altar, laying hands on those who have special needs (such as healing or freedom from addiction), as well as those who simply want more of God's love, joy, peace, power and presence in their lives. What joy Denise and I feel when our three children choose to wait in line for prayer! We have seen Isabelle, Christine and Samuel filled with the Holy Spirit over and over again. They are often the first to run to the altar to worship or volunteer to pray for a hurting soul. They have received more through prayer, but they also pour out more.

During our early years as a family, there was a great lack of impartation prayer. It has become a regular practice, only in the past five years—and what a difference it has made. We have seen with our own eyes the great things God has imparted to our children through us, when we have laid hands on them. Our prayers have force now. They are not empty words that travel no farther than the ceiling. We have faith that our prayers change our children's lives. We believe it and so do they.

At one service, Isabelle—following the example of Elisha in 2 Kings 2:9—asked for a double portion of my spirit. I have often said, "I can't give what I don't have." Only God could answer that one!

Even though we must go through a certain amount of self-examination and preparation, we certainly don't have to wait until we are perfect, in order to impart to our children or to be used by God in other ways. Of course, if that were a requirement, none of us would ever be qualified! Once your heart is right before the Lord and you've truly surrendered yourself to Him—and once He has filled you and you have something valuable to pour into your children—go home and pray for them. Lay hands on them and impart to them.

At first they may look at you as if you were from another planet or they may seem bored, exasperated or embarrassed. Don't be intimidated by their response. Don't argue, accuse, condemn or loose your composure. Don't take yourself too seriously; hang on to your sense of humor. Just keep covering them in prayer, openly loving them and speaking positive, encouraging words over them. In time, they will want what you have. It may not happen overnight, but eventually, the seeds you sow in faith will produce a harvest of righteousness. If your children are younger, these prayers can become part of their routine. You do not have to close your eyes or play a worship CD in the background for your child to receive the impact of your faith.

TRANSFORMATION KEY 5: MODELING IS SETTING THE RIGHT EXAMPLE

We touched on this subject earlier, but the importance of modeling—imparting desired attitudes, behavior and character traits through example—can't be stressed enough. The saying that goes, "I can't hear your words, because your actions are speaking so loudly," is especially relevant to the relationship between a child and his or her parent.

Never forget that your children are watching you. Even when you think they aren't looking, they are. They are noticing whether you practice what you preach. They are observing whether the way you behave before and after church (when only your family is there to see you) lines up with the way you behave during church. They are listening to the way you talk about your neighbors, your in-laws and your co-workers. They are forming images of your relationship with your mate. They are taking note of how you respond to success, adversity, temptation, victory, injustice, gossip and failure. They are learning from your example: how to deal with anger, love, sorrow, fear and other emotions.

Even Paul the apostle encouraged believers, as he wrote, *"Imitate me, just as I also imitate Christ"* (1 Corinthians 11:1). Paul understood the impact of his decisions and actions. He welcomed the fact that he was a role model. He embraced his role as a spiritual father.

TRANSFORMATION KEY 6: TEACH YOUR CHILDREN WELL

A few years ago I realized that I did not spend a lot of time mentoring my children. I lived out my faith and preached it, but I seldom spent any time, intentionally teaching life principles to them. I needed to become a Proverbs 1 father:

Proverbs 1:8
My son, hear the instruction of your father,
And do not forsake the law of your mother . . .

Solomon took time to instruct his son in the principles of wisdom, but I was neglecting to do so. The Holy Spirit clearly showed me my lack, while at the same time, He was also convicting Denise of her responsibility. (I will let her tell you her side of the story in another book.) After all, Solomon admonishes his son to remember what he has been taught by both his father and his mother. I'm not saying we have to give our children a daily lecture, but we need to be alert to the teaching opportunities that arise naturally, from day to day. Deuteronomy 6:6-9 powerfully illustrates the biblical impartation that we are to practice with our children:

"And these words which I command you today shall be in your heart. You shall teach them diligently to your children, and shall talk of them when you sit in your house, when you walk by the way, when you lie down, and when you rise up. You shall bind them as a sign on your hand, and they shall be as frontlets between your eyes. You shall write them on the doorposts of your house and on your gates."

The Power of the Word

Hebrews 4:12
For the word of God is living and powerful, and sharper than any two-edged sword, piercing even to the division of soul and spirit, and of joints and marrow, and is a discerner of the thoughts and intents of the heart.

Let's unwrap this Scripture, to give us a road map for our children First of all, we must fill our hearts with truth and pour it out in a relaxed, daily setting. If God's Word is not part of you, your efforts to impart will look fake and sound forced. However, if you have hidden the Word inside of you, ask God for the wisdom to teach your children about God and His Word. The practice of Scripture memorization and recitation were also already a huge part of Jesus' culture.

Psalm 119:11
*Your word I have hidden in my heart,
That I might not sin against You.*

Jeremiah 31:33
But this is the covenant that I will make with the house of Israel after those days, says the Lord: I will put My law in their minds, and write it on their hearts; and I will be their God, and they shall be My people.

The Power of Your Story

Revelation 12:11
"And they overcame him by the blood of the Lamb and by the word of their testimony, and they did not love their lives to the death."

Another way to impart wisdom and insight to our children is by using parables, like Jesus did. Parables are merely short, simple stories that help explain profound truths. With a little creativity, we can make up modern parables for our children, by using everyday situations and events. Search local, Christian bookstores for ideas. They are a great resource for object lessons and projects that will bring the Word to life.

I have discovered that my own, personal stories are great story-telling fodder. My kids have loved my stories through the years. I've tried to remain transparent and very human about my past and my present situations. I'm sure that I've repeated them so many times that my kids can repeat them verbatim. Sometimes they tease me about this tool, but I know that it has been effective.

This intentional form of transferring is a step that takes wisdom and timing. It also requires a close relationship with your children. We must be genuinely interested in their lives. We need to learn to listen to them, without reacting in a judgmental, overly-emotional manner, and we must hear their feelings, as well as the facts about a situation. We must learn when to teach and when to be silent. I have discovered a few key moments in a child's day that seem to work quite well:

- **Driving to and from school or other destinations.** Turn off the radio and cell phones, so that you can talk, play games and laugh.
- **A five-minute breakfast devotional.** Read a short passage from the Word and discuss it, or memorize a Scripture together.
- **A prayer before school.** Take a minute to hold your child's hand and pray a blessing over him or her, right before they exit the car.
- **A bedtime devotional.** A short time of prayer, coupled with a reading from Scripture is a great way to end the day.

Try to make these times interactive. Let them ask questions and even divert from the discussion. It will not be perfect. Be patient and find out what works and doesn't. Every child is different. I have known some parents who feel guilty if they don't hold mini-revival meetings each day. Those expectations are not realistic. It places too much of a burden on the children and the parents. Just look for little windows of time during the day and take advantage of them. Each one will open up your child to God and, little by little, he or she will be given insights and revelations.

Teach Them by Committing to a Great Church

Another key way that we taught our children was by plugging into a great church. In the Goulet household, Sunday church, Sunday school and Wednesday Bible study have all been a priority. Yes, we did force our children to go, but we were rarely tested, because we modeled faithful attendance their entire lives. Even before I was a senior pastor, we were committed to a local body of believers. Being part of the body of Christ (i.e. the local church body) has always been important to us. I believe that modeling healthy church involvement and commitment has made a huge difference in our lives. Make sure that you find a church that has great children and youth leaders. It needs to be one of your highest priorities. Make sure that the leaders are real, transparent and loving to all children. Find a vibrant church that loves God and people. Then get involved.

We exposed our children to all kinds of ministry opportunities and adventures. They have fed the homeless, served in Sunday school and traveled with me to India. They have prayed for the sick and prophesied over people. They have been involved in the Royal Rangers and Missionettes, along with their youth group. Churches are never perfect, because people aren't perfect; however, commitment is required to turn immature children into world-changers.

TRANSFORMATION KEY 7: BUILD YOUR FAMILY UP WITH YOUR WORDS

When we are not intentionally instructing our children, our words are a powerful means of impartation and transformation. Ephesians 4:29 warns us to be careful how we use words:

Let no corrupt word proceed out of your mouth, but what is good for necessary edification, that it may impart grace to the hearers.

Our homes should be places where grace is imparted through open communication. Does that describe your home? Do your children love to be home, because you speak graciously to them? Do your words build them up, according to their needs? Do the things you say benefit your mate and children or is your home a place where words are used to wound, intimidate and accuse? When your children mess up, are they greeted with belittling remarks, sarcastic comments or outbursts of rage? Granted, we have all become impatient with our children at times and said things we shouldn't have. We need grace as parents. So, we should never hesitate to ask for our children's forgiveness when we have been at fault.

Our words should *"impart grace to the hearers"* (Ephesians 4:29). They should be spoken with truth and love.

Ephesians 4:15-16
. . . but, speaking the truth in love, may grow up in all things into Him who is the head—Christ—from whom the whole body, joined and knit together by what every joint supplies, according to the effective working by which every part does its share, causes growth of the body for the edifying of itself in love.

I've often encouraged parents and couples to speak the truth in love and not with army boots on. Every word you speak is an important and powerful tool of impartation; we can never learn too much about how to use them. In the next chapter we will address the need to teach our children principles and truths that will equip them to face life as overcomers.

Questions to Make You Think

Q: What teaching tools have been most effective with your children?

Q: What teaching strategy do you want to implement with your children?

Q: What qualities do you look for in a church?

Q: How can you get you and your children involved in your church of choice?

CHAPTER 10

TOPICS TO TEACH YOUR CHILDREN

The question that puzzles so many parents is what they should teach their children. What life lessons are important enough to prioritize? Many parents leave life lessons up to the church, school or even Sesame Street. Unfortunately, that tendency is quite a gamble. Living in Las Vegas, I know a little bit about gambling. I'd like to dedicate a few pages to a list of priority subjects that will empower your child to become an incredible adult.

13 GEMS TO TEACH YOUR CHILDREN

1. **TEACH THEM THE WORD OF GOD.** It is living and active. Teach them to love it.

Hebrews 4:12
For the word of God is living and powerful, and sharper than any two-edged sword, piercing even to the division of soul and spirit, and of joints and marrow, and is a discerner of the thoughts and intents of the heart.

2. **Teach them to worship God.** Teach them to appreciate the various forms of worship and music.

2 Corinthians 10:4-5
For the weapons of our warfare are not carnal but mighty in God for pulling down strongholds, casting down arguments and every high thing that exalts itself against the knowledge of God, bringing every thought into captivity to the obedience of Christ . . .

3. **Teach them to love God and love people.** The Bible says those are the two greatest commandments.

Mark 12:30-31
"And you shall love the LORD your God with all your heart, with all your soul, with all your mind, and with all your strength.' This is the first commandment. And the second, like it, is this: 'You shall love your neighbor as yourself.' There is no other commandment greater than these."

4. **Teach them about their bodies and their sexuality.** A great resource is Dr. Richard Dobbins' book *Teaching Your Children About Sex.*

5. **Teach them that their potential is without limit.** The following illustration will help them understand how to live out their divine potential.

Dr. Richard Dobbins "Model of the Mind" provides a visual aid to help us understand the primary method that God communicates with you and I. I have simplified and modified it for our theme. According to Dr. Dobbins' teaching, God speaks to our minds on a daily basis, stimulating us to think thoughts and make choices that will lead us to our divine potential. God's vision for your life will only be accomplished when your thoughts and choices change, in order to fulfill God's vision for you.

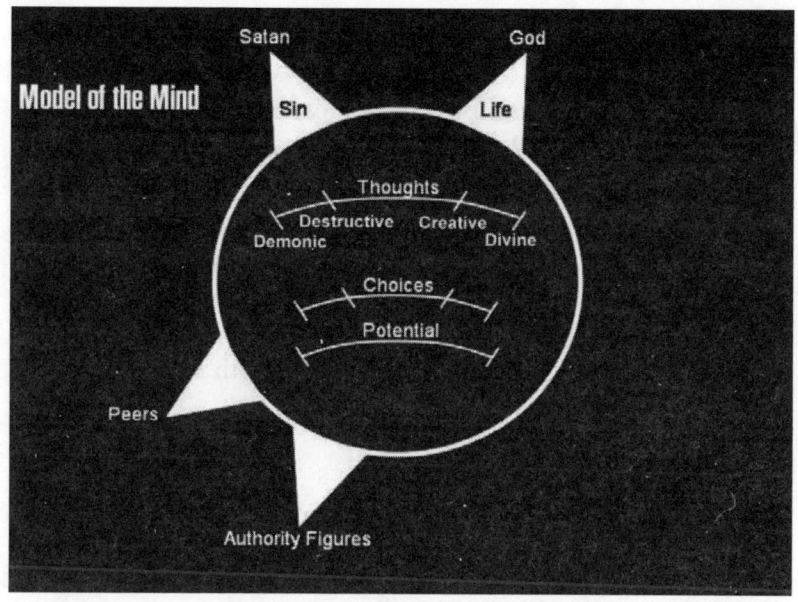

Satan also speaks to your mind daily; he stimulates your mind to think thoughts and make choices that will lead you to your demonic potential. Are you fulfilling your divine potential, or are you slipping into Satan's will for your life? Can you think about people who have reached their creative and divine potential? It is certainly not difficult to list those who lived out their destructive or demonic potential (e.g. Suddam Hussein, Hitler). Teach your children this concept and help them understand that they can reach their divine potential.

6. **TEACH THEM TO KEEP A CLEAN HEART.** Dr. Richard Dobbins once said, "You do not live with the facts of your life, but the interpretation of the facts of your life." We receive most information through our senses, consciously. All our facts are items, filtered through our unconscious reservoir of positively-charged and negatively-charged memories of events and circumstances. Your conscious mind is like the software in your

computer. Your unconscious mind is your hard drive. In most cases the problems in our lives are caused by faulty hardware, filled with viruses and bugs. The Holy Spirit wants to help us clean out our hard drives, so that clear visions may be re-established. Again: "We do not live with the facts of our lives, but the interpretation of the facts of our lives." Here's a little checklist that will help you coach your child through emotional mine fields:

- Forgive all those who have hurt you or with whom you have been upset or angry.

Ephesians 4:26
"Be angry, and do not sin": do not let the sun go down on your wrath . . .

- Ask God to forgive you for bitterness, jealousy, envy or any other emotional toxic wastes.

Ephesians 4:31
Let all bitterness, wrath, anger, clamor, and evil speaking be put away from you, with all malice.

- Get it all out. Write a letter that you will never send to the person that hurt you. Confide in a trusted parent. Go for a long walk. Anger can be diffused without hurting other people.

- Renounce any other spirit that would like to fill your heart.

Romans 8:15
For you did not receive the spirit of bondage again to fear, but you received the Spirit of adoption by whom we cry out, "Abba, Father."

- Teach them about the vat (illustrated on the following page). The vat represents the process by which we interpret everything we see, hear, feel and sense.

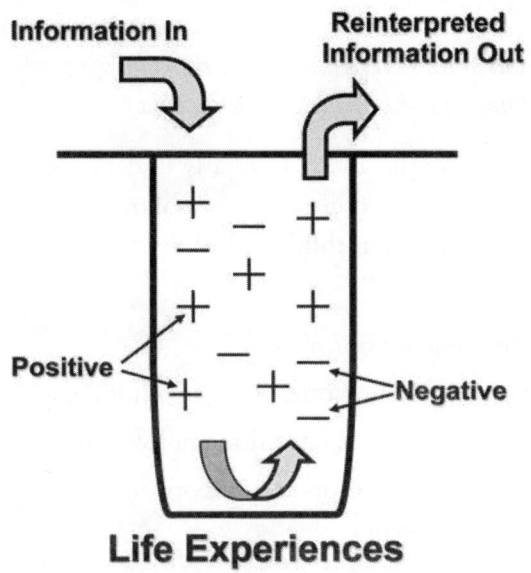

Life Experiences

1 Corinthians 13:12
For now we see in a mirror, dimly, but then face to face. Now I know in part, but then I shall know just as I also am known.

In other words: We interpret everything that we receive through our senses. We filter all incoming information through the positive and negative memories that we store in our minds. These memories are both conscious and unconscious. These unconscious and conscious memories filter everything we experience. The Bible calls this process "the heart."

Jeremiah 17:9
"The heart is deceitful above all things,
And desperately wicked;
Who can know it?"

Luke 6:45
"A good man out of the good treasure of his heart brings forth good; and an evil man out of the evil treasure of his heart brings forth evil. For out of the abundance of the heart his mouth speaks."

In order to have the ability to clearly understand and interpret our everyday lives, it is crucial that we allow the Holy Spirit to change the way we speak, think and understand. The Holy Spirit will:

✔ Help us confront our past.

✔ Reinterpret our memories from an adult perspective.

✔ Process emotionally-charged memories through prayer.

✔ Seek the help of pastors, counselors or friends, to overcome troubling memories.

7. **Teach them how to resolve conflict.** (Life will be full of conflicts.) Equip them with the tools to practice resolving conflict. Such as:

• Speak the truth in love.

Ephesians 4:15-16
. . . but, speaking the truth in love, may grow up in all things into Him who is the head—Christ—from whom the whole body, joined and knit together by what every joint supplies, according to the effective working by which every part does its share, causes growth of the body for the edifying of itself in love.

• If someone hurts them:

Matthew 18:15-17
"Moreover if your brother sins against you, go and tell him his fault between you and him alone. If he hears you, you have gained your brother. But if he will not hear, take with you one or two more, that 'by the mouth of two or three witnesses every word may be established.' And

if he refuses to hear them, tell it to the church. But if he refuses even to hear the church, let him be to you like a heathen and a tax collector."

- If someone is mad at them:

Matthew 5:23-24
"Therefore if you bring your gift to the altar, and there remember that your brother has something against you, leave your gift there before the altar, and go your way. First be reconciled to your brother, and then come and offer your gift."

8. TEACH THEM HOW TO FORGIVE.

Matthew 6:14-15
"For if you forgive men their trespasses, your heavenly Father will also forgive you. But if you do not forgive men their trespasses, neither will your Father forgive your trespasses."

There are three steps to forgiving others:

- The act. It's like brushing your teeth. All you need to do is say, "I forgive (insert name here), in the name of Jesus." When we are hurt, infection quickly sets in. The infection is anger and/or bitterness. Forgiveness disinfects the cut. The prayer of healing helps the emotional wound. After your child forgives, pray that God will heal the hurt he or she has suffered.

- The process.

Matthew 18:21-22
Then Peter came to Him and said, "Lord, how often shall my brother sin against me, and I forgive him? Up to seven times?" Jesus said to him, "I do not say to you, up to seven times, but up to seventy times seven."

The response of Jesus demonstrated the need to keep forgiving, until the pain or anger is no longer connected to the memory. Every time the anger or hurt returns we are called to keep forgiving, up to four-hundred and ninety times. This counting is also counter-productive, because perfect love does not keep track of wrongs suffered (1 Corinthians 13:5 NIV).

- The state of forgiveness is achieved when we can think of the person or event and it no longer causes any more pain or anger. We discover that, even though we never really forget the memory, we are no longer connected to it by the strong, emotional baggage. The process has reached its ultimate goal and we are then free.

9. **TEACH THEM THE RELATIONSHIP BETWEEN THEIR THOUGHTS, FEELINGS AND ACTIONS.** I call that the "Circle of Process". The Circle of Process is based upon "The Awareness Wheel" by Miller P. and Miller S.

Through thousands of hours of counseling and study, I am convinced that insight and understanding are two powerful tools to help our sons and daughters process their thoughts and feelings. They should be able to answer the big questions of life, such as: Why do I feel this way? Why do I keep doing things that undermine my success? Why do I sabotage my intentions?

The Circle of Process

- **Something happens.** It could be a sound, experience, a word or even an image. It could be a car accident or divorce.

- **Something is received or experienced.** You hear, see, smell, taste or feel the something that just happened. You experience the event.

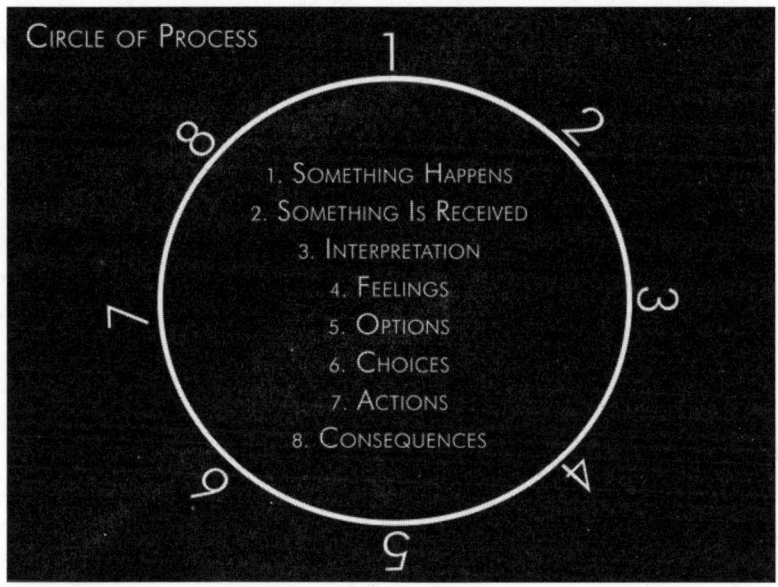

CIRCLE OF PROCESS

1. SOMETHING HAPPENS
2. SOMETHING IS RECEIVED
3. INTERPRETATION
4. FEELINGS
5. OPTIONS
6. CHOICES
7. ACTIONS
8. CONSEQUENCES

- **Interpretation.** You interpret what you receive with your five senses. As Christians, we also believe that we have a sixth sense that is spiritual. Our sixth sense can also receive expressions or discernment.

- **Feelings.** Our feelings are not based on facts, circumstances, events or other people. They are based on our interpretation of the facts, events or circumstances of our lives.

- **Options.** What is our first reaction to a particular feeling? Remember when your mother told you to count to ten, when you were angry? She was trying to help you with your impulse control. Driven by the energy of the emotions, a person will look at a menu of options: What can I do? What should I do?

- **Choices.** Once the options are reviewed, a person will make some type of choice from their menu of responses.

- **Actions.** After they choose a solution, action, plan or strategy, they must implement their choice.

<u>Romans 7:15</u>
For what I am doing, I do not understand. For what I will to do, that I do not practice; but what I hate, that I do.

- **Consequences.** Inevitably, every one of us will live with the consequences of our decisions and actions—which leads us right back to "something happens". We will receive the consequences of our choices and actions.

<u>Galatians 6:7</u>
Do not be deceived, God is not mocked; for whatever a man sows, that he will also reap.

A Vicious Cycle

Perhaps you can see how this process can actually become a vicious cycle. Once your interpretation is wrong or distorted, it will affect every part of your life. It's difficult to break free from this downward spiral. In counseling theory there are several treatment approaches that were designed to help people who are caught in negative cycles. Behavior modification targets the behavior of a person, through rewards or pain. Others try to help teenagers create a list of decisions and consequences. Still others will try to change a persons thought life, by inserting positive, life-empowering declarations.

I have always believed that, if you attack the roots, the weeds won't return. With the Circle of Process in mind, the root of the problem is often an interpretation of the events of their lives. We cannot change the past of a hurting person, but we can help them reinterpret it. As a leader of your family, you must help your family process the hurtful events of life. If you teach them how to interpret death, failures, sickness, rejection and tragedies you will empower them to overcome. Your children will watch your interpretations and reactions to life. In other words: Your words and actions will teach them how to interpret life.

Reinterpret the Events of Your Life

The apostle Paul was a master at reinterpreting trials, setbacks, rejections and persecutions:

Philippians 3:7-8
But what things were gain to me, these I have counted loss for Christ. Yet indeed I also count all things loss for the excellence of the knowledge of Christ Jesus my Lord, for whom I have suffered the loss of all things, and count them as rubbish, that I may gain Christ . . .

Romans 8:28
And we know that all things work together for good to those who love God, to those who are the called according to His purpose.

Philippians 1:12
But I want you to know, brethren, that the things which happened to me have actually turned out for the furtherance of the gospel . . .

Romans 8:18
For I consider that the sufferings of this present time are not worthy to be compared with the glory which shall be revealed in us.

Paul learned the secret of an indestructible life; he learned the secret that created a firm foundation. If you can teach yourself and your family to interpret life with the help of the Holy Spirit, you too will build a generational blessing for your family and others who learn from you. Moms and dads, you can give your children a gift that will guarantee an amazing life: the power to interpret.

10. **Teach them to honor your parents and grandparents.** Teach your kids to love and respect them.

Ephesians 6:2
"Honor your father and mother," which is the first commandment with promise . . .

I had amazing grandparents. As the fifth child in our family, I did not get to spend many years with them; however, my memories are very positive. I have a huge respect for the legacy that was left in the three grandparents that I knew as a child.

11. **Teach your children to serve others, especially the less fortunate.**

Matthew 22:37-39
Jesus said to him, "'You shall love the LORD your God with all your heart, with all your soul, and with all your mind.' This is the first and great commandment. And the second is like it: 'You shall love your neighbor as yourself.'"

12. **Teach your children to be givers.** True wealth is not what you accumulate; it is what you manage to give away.

Luke 6:38
"Give, and it will be given to you: good measure, pressed down, shaken together, and running over will be put into your bosom. For with the same measure that you use, it will be measured back to you."

13. **Teach them about building a strong marriage.** If you are married, prioritize your marriage. Your kids will love you for it. If you are a single parent and thinking about marriage, pick the right person who you can build a strong family with.

MARRIAGE TIPS

Denise and I have been married for twenty-eight years and I thought I would share with you a few little secrets we have held in our hearts, that have kept us close throughout the years:

- Go out on weekly dates; romance her and spoil her with love, time and affection.

- Find out your spouse's love language and speak it often. Mine is touch and words of affirmation. Denise's is time and acts of service.

- Husbands, pour love on your wives on a daily basis. Wives, it is important to show respect to your husband, as you love him back (Ephesians 5:22).

- Don't let the sun go down on your anger.

    a.) Resolve your conflicts before the end of the day. Speak the truth in love rather than in anger (Ephesians 4:15).

    b.) Forgive all offenses and hurts, as often as they arrive.

- Don't nag or take revenge. Let the Holy Spirit speak to them.

- Take at least one vacation a year, just for the two of you. Take another one with your kids, if you can. Day trips are big memory-makers. They are quite an experience and they are fun. I remember going to see the boats on the river, as a child. I even recall going to the airport to watch the planes fly out. My dad and mom were doing their best to give us family memories that would bless us. All these memories are stored in my mind and heart. I am so grateful for their efforts to bond our family.

- Listen to your spouse daily. Work on good communication techniques.

- In an argument, don't attack your mate's character. If you do, stop and ask for forgiveness.

- Believe the best of your spouse. Help them fly for Jesus. Lift up your mate in the eyes of others. Never expose their weaknesses to others, through sarcasm or anger. Build them up in the eyes of your family.

- Read a book on marriage and relationships at least every year. You can keep learning great insights, instead of growing stale.

- Work out three or four times a week and watch what you eat. Dress and take time to make yourself pretty, ladies. Men, don't be slobs. Look fit and handsome for your spouse.

- Don't take your mate for granted. Spoil your husband or wife.

- Don't be cheap. Divorce is very costly. Be generous with your spouse, your kids and your church.

- Laugh a lot! Life is hard. So, laugh at a funny movie or the events of the day.

- Stay humble and teachable. Don't be proud or stubborn. You don't always have to be right.

- Set your priorities for your marriage and family: God, marriage, kids and then work.

- Find a great church, job, neighborhood and school. This will be the environment that you choose for your children to learn from.

- Pick your associates and associations carefully. Remember that your associations will determine your destination.

1 Corinthians 15:33 (NIV)
Do not be misled: "Bad company corrupts good character."

Questions to Make You Think

Q: What family traditions do you want to pass down to your children?

Q: Have you taught your children about finances, careers and choosing a mate? If not, what principles are important to you?

Q: How strong is your marriage?

Q: How much have you invested in your marriage?

Q: Do your words strengthen your children or are they a weapon?

Q: What words could you express, to help your children?

CHAPTER 11

12 STEPS TO SPIRITUAL TRANSFORMATION

When people walk into your home, what is their first impression? I'm not talking about your furniture or decorations. I'm referring to the feeling and spirit that is most noticeable. You might call it "the atmosphere" that your home projects to others who visit. My two daughters and one son-in-law are realtors. We've had fun investing in homes and home-shopping on many occasions. We couldn't wait to leave certain homes, because the atmosphere was funky. Have you ever felt this way in a home?

As a young boy, I remember loving to be at my friend Karl's house. He was Lebanese. His parents were cool. Their food was awesome. I loved the atmosphere there. They made me feel comfortable. That's what I'm talking about. Whether you know it or not, your home is full of emotional and spiritual elements that will touch the lives who enter it. What did you receive from your childhood home and family?

Revival in the Home

Joel 2:28
"And it shall come to pass afterward
That I will pour out My Spirit on all flesh;
Your sons and your daughters shall prophesy,
Your old men shall dream dreams,
Your young men shall see visions."

God's plan has always been to have entire families in spiritual health and wholeness. Unfortunately, many families I have encountered are living far below God's ideal. It doesn't matter how far off-base your family might be. The following 12 steps will help you impart a spiritual revival that will birth long-term change.

1. **Examine yourself.** If we are going to take the role of imparter seriously, the first step is to examine ourselves. Are you emotionally and relationally healthy? (If not, one way to begin the road toward spiritual health and wholeness is to go through the Breakthrough Series. See www.iclv.com to purchase a copy.) Are you spiritually healthy? Our spiritual health will determine the nature and power of our prayers. If we are spiritually lukewarm, in rebellion against God or indulging in habitual sin, what can we possibly pass on to our children that would be of value? Ask the Lord to help you see the truth about yourself, even if it hurts. Whatever the results are of your quest, take the following steps in order to improve and maintain your spiritual health.

Psalm 139:23
Search me, O God, and know my heart;
Try me, and know my anxieties . . .

2. **Ask God for a truly repentant, broken and contrite heart, for greater spiritual hunger and passion as well as the desire and the ability to be pure, holy and utterly surrendered to Him.**

Psalm 51:17
The sacrifices of God are a broken spirit,
A broken and a contrite heart—
These, O God, You will not despise.

3. **Ask Him to fill you with faith, wisdom, boldness and love.** Above all, ask for a desperate, all-consuming love for Him. As parents, we are the thermostats of spiritual intensity in our homes. If we want to see our children on fire for God and serving Him wholeheartedly, we need to start by warming up our own spiritual climates. Our hearts and our homes have to become greenhouses for the transference of spiritual gifts.

Ephesians 2:8
For by grace you have been saved through faith, and that not of your-
selves; it is the gift of God . . .

4. **Throw yourself into seeking God and He will fill you.** Pursue Him in practical ways. Ask Him to pour a heart of hunger and passion into you. *"For it is God who works in you both, to will and to do for His good pleasure"* (Philippians 2:13).

Jeremiah 29:13
"And you will seek Me and find Me, when you search for Me with all
your heart."

5. **Ask a great man or woman of God to lay hands on you, in order to impart spiritual blessing.** Put yourself under the leadership of your pastor. Respond to the Holy Spirit, His

Word and anointed preaching. Be open to receive a touch from heaven.

1 Timothy 4:14
Do not neglect the gift that is in you, which was given to you by prophecy with the laying on of the hands of the eldership.

6. Get involved in a discipleship program or a weekly Bible study at your home church.

2 Timothy 2:15
Be diligent to present yourself approved to God, a worker who does not need to be ashamed, rightly dividing the word of truth.

7. Have a daily quiet-time with God, that includes prayer, praise, worship and study of Scripture. Learn to be still and listen for His voice.

Isaiah 55:6
Seek the LORD while He may be found,
Call upon Him while He is near.

8. Fast regularly. I started fasting on a regular basis over fifteen years ago. There is no doubt in my mind that the fruit in our family and our church has a direct correlation to the discipline of fasting and prayer. Fasting has also taken center stage in the most difficult seasons of our lives.

Matthew 17:21
"However, this kind does not go out except by prayer and fasting."

9. Fill yourself with spiritual gems. Read literature and listen to music, sermons and teachings that uplift, educate, inspire and edify you. (Make sure they are biblical and produced by reliable men and women of God.)

James 1:5
If any of you lacks wisdom, let him ask of God, who gives to all liberally and without reproach, and it will be given to him.

10. **Stay away from any activity or entertainment that might come between you and the Lord.** Stay sensitive to the Holy Spirit. He will cause you to feel uncomfortable in different scenarios. Be alert to these leadings.

Hebrews 3:7-8
Therefore, as the Holy Spirit says:
"Today, if you will hear His voice,
Do not harden your hearts as in the rebellion,
In the day of trial in the wilderness . . ."

11. **Pray for discernment.** Learn to be sensitive and obedient to the promptings of the Holy Spirit. The gifts of the Holy Spirit are for everyone. God wants to bless you with His gifts. Revelatory gifts—like the discerning of spirits, wisdom and words of knowledge—are so important for a family setting.

Galatians 5:16
I say then: Walk in the Spirit, and you shall not fulfill the lust of the flesh.

Revival in your family can produce life-long changes. God's goal for any outpouring of His Spirit is generational transformation. Do you want God to touch your family or transform it? I don't know about you, but I want both.

12. **Ask God to fill you with His power.** In my book *The Five Powers of God,* I teach that, behind the English word for "power" in the New Testament, there lies five Greek words with distinct meanings and purposes. God knows which power you need, whether it be dynamite, authority, energy, strength or

dominion. He will fill you with the ones you need the most for your breakthrough.

Luke 10:19

Behold, I give you the authority to trample on serpents and scorpions, and over all the power of the enemy, and nothing shall by any means hurt you.

CHAPTER 12

IT'S TIME TO THINK
ABOUT GENERATIONS

When God wants to move in the earth realm, He looks for a family to use as a gate for His blessings and plans. Throughout the Old Testament we see God using a family for generations and generations. God functions in relationship to individuals and their families. In Acts we are promised that, when one person is saved, God's will is to save the entire family.

Acts 16:31
So they said, "Believe on the Lord Jesus Christ, and you will be saved, you and your household."

There are three important revelations that God has shown me about family units being the gate through which heaven can enter.

1. **God starts with one person.** God is always looking for people who want a relationship with Him. When He finds that person, He enters into a covenant (i.e. an agreement that is

mutually binding) with that person, which will require something on both sides. There are many examples of God's pattern of touching one person, to touch a family, to touch a city or to change a nation. God always starts with one. Will you be the person who God uses to touch a family? Here are a few classic examples of this principle:

• God chose Abram.

Genesis 12:2-3
"I will make you a great nation;
I will bless you
And make your name great;
And you shall be a blessing."

• God chose Jacob.

Genesis 28:13-14
And behold, the LORD stood above it and said: "I am the LORD God of Abraham your father and the God of Isaac; the land on which you lie I will give to you and your descendants. Also your descendants shall be as the dust of the earth; you shall spread abroad to the west and the east, to the north and the south; and in you and in your seed all the families of the earth shall be blessed."

• God chose Gideon.

Judges 6:12
And the Angel of the LORD appeared to him, and said to him, "The LORD is with you, you mighty man of valor!"

• God chose David.

1 Samuel 16:13
Then Samuel took the horn of oil and anointed him in the midst of his brothers; and the Spirit of the LORD came upon David from that day forward. So Samuel arose and went to Ramah.

- God chose Mary.

Luke 1:28
And having come in, the angel said to her, "Rejoice, highly favored one, the Lord is with you; blessed are you among women!"

2. **One person becomes a gatekeeper for the entire family.** You are a gatekeeper for your family. God is looking for a godly man, woman or young person to serve as gatekeepers. You can become the person that God uses to transform your family, city, generation and nation.

- Jabez stood out in his family, so God answered his prayer and blessed him.

1 Chronicles 4:10
And Jabez called on the God of Israel saying, "Oh, that You would bless me indeed, and enlarge my territory, that Your hand would be with me, and that You would keep me from evil, that I may not cause pain!" So God granted him what he requested.

- Abram was chosen as a gatekeeper.

Genesis 12:3
"I will bless those who bless you,
And I will curse him who curses you;
And in you all the families of the earth shall be blessed."

- Joseph was chosen to transform Egypt and save his family.

Genesis 50:20
"But as for you, you meant evil against me; but God meant it for good, in order to bring it about as it is this day, to save many people alive."

Gatekeepers are people who catch heaven's attention by holiness, faith, obedience, kindness, sacrifice and faithfulness. Their decisions and actions affect the immediate family and future generations. Denise and I made a firm decision at the beginning of our marriage, that we would be an example to both of our families and to all those who surround us. We made some tough choices, simply to be gatekeepers. We decided to shut the door on the following:

- Alcohol use. Even though both of our families allow alcohol in the home, we felt that we wanted to eliminate the possibility that we would lead someone else astray.

- Smoking.

- Movies that contain foul language and nudity.

- Gossip.

- Bitterness. Forgiveness and reconciliation had to happen before the sun went down.

- Excessive TV. We limited time and did not order premium channels.

- Uncensored Internet. Filters were placed on our computers, to minimize the risk of pornography and computers were placed in rooms without doors.

- Non-Christian music. My wife and I play Christian music in our home. We believe that our home is a type of sanctuary. If our children want to listen to non-Christian music we allow them to make this choice; however, the content has its limits.

- Denise and I have broken all generational curses, through prayer and agreement. Doors were firmly shut.

- Disrespect in our home. Respect is a big issue in our family. Although we have had some pretty interesting conversations at times, we always brought closure to disagreements and fostered forgiveness and repentance.

These are just a few of the doors that were deliberately shut by my wife and I. We have always felt responsible to be the gatekeepers. Sin would try to enter through other gates, but we have been committed that, with God's help, it would not enter through us.

In Matthew, Jesus empowers Peter and the disciples with the ability to bind and loose.

<u>Matthew 16:19</u>
"And I will give you the keys of the kingdom of heaven, and whatever you bind on earth will be bound in heaven, and whatever you loose on earth will be loosed in heaven."

In this context I believe that it includes the authority to open and shut gates. The gates that my wife and I have tried to open in our home are the following:

- Good boundaries. Our babies were trained to sleep in their own rooms at a specific bedtime. Our bedroom was our private place. Although they could knock on our door any time, for extra love, assurance or comfort, we made sure that these boundaries were firm. The life of the couple is so important; don't neglect it because of sloppy boundaries. There are, of course, exceptions to this rule. When our children struggled with illness, we took whatever steps we needed to properly nurture and care for their needs.

- Encouragement. During our birthday and anniversary celebrations, our family traditionally encourages everyone to share positive memories or words of encouragement. It is our goal to bathe them with presents, cards and kind words. Our gate of "life words" is not limited to birthdays. We've always tried to be encouraging and affirming on a daily basis. Someone once preached that, for every word of correction, ten words of affirmation should be given. I agree.

• Faithful church attendance. Even before Denise and I entered full-time ministry, we attended church on Sundays and Wednesday nights. Our children, of course, came also. We've tried to make church important to them, but also fun and relevant.

• Service. Our three children have come with us on various missions and outreach trips. The most noticeable trip was to India. I am a firm believer in the importance of serving others. If your children can start this habit young, it will be with them for their whole lives. Our three children are very involved, serving the local church.

Three years ago we opened our home up to two African teenagers who were seeking a better life in America. Blessed with height, they were seeking future college education and basketball experience. Our family fell in love with these two boys from Rwanda. They have become an important part of our family. When they moved in, my son opened up his room to them. Can you imagine the commotion with three tall (each over six feet), young men, all in a small room? It was crazy. What really grabbed me was the fact that my son volunteered to share his room. Volunteering, serving and giving has always been a huge part of the Goulet family.

Our two African sons got into the rhythm of serving. It's their last summer before college and they chose to volunteer at the church for the summer. Isn't that great? The open gate impacted them and now they are setting an example.

• Giving to God and others.

<u>Luke 6:38</u>

"Give, and it will be given to you: good measure, pressed down, shaken together, and running over will be put into your bosom. For with the same measure that you use, it will be measured back to you."

My wife and I have given our tithes since the beginning of our marriage, even when things were financially tough. My wife led the way in this department for many years. Through our twenty-eight years of marriage and sixteen years of leading ICLV through expansion, God has empowered us to give more aggressively.

My friend Dr. Marocco challenged me in this area, about nine years ago. He asked me a question that shocked me: "Paul, what are you giving to God this year?" I had never really thought about that until his question irritated me into reconsidering my views on giving. He then told me how much he gave the previous year. After I digested his question, I quoted Matthew 6:3-4, saying, *"But when you do a charitable deed, do not let your left hand know what your right hand is doing, that your charitable deed may be in secret; and your Father who sees in secret will Himself reward you openly."* Then I asked, "Didn't Jesus teach against talking about our giving like this?" His answer led Denise and I on a new journey of giving and reaping that has changed our family. He said, "Paul, Jesus was talking about alms. Alms is giving to the poor. You don't talk about it, because you don't want to embarrass the poor."

After this discussion, Denise and I set our first giving goal for the coming year. To our surprise, we surpassed it by far. Since that day we have given a home, cars, our entire savings, my paychecks (for eleven months of last year) and Denise has given up her paychecks for this year. I have to admit that, not only are we blessed beyond our expectations, but our children have become crazy givers to God and others. It's so exciting to see my own children leading their families with the gate of giving and leading the way.

There are so many more gates that a mom, dad or teen can open to their families: excellence, knowledge, purity, character, faith, courage, kindness or hospitality. What gates have you opened for your family? Everyone in a family can become a gatekeeper. Being one is not limited to a mother or father, but it is easier to lead from the top. Great examples of those who led from the middle or rear of the pack are:

- Gideon

Judges 6:15
So he said to Him, "O my Lord, how can I save Israel? Indeed my clan is the weakest in Manasseh, and I am the least in my father's house."

- David

2 Samuel 7:8
"Now therefore, thus shall you say to My servant David, 'Thus says the LORD of hosts: I took you from the sheepfold, from following the sheep, to be ruler over My people, over Israel.'"

- Rahab

Hebrews 11:31
By faith the harlot Rahab did not perish with those who did not believe, when she had received the spies with peace.

- Timothy

1 Timothy 4:12
Let no one despise your youth, but be an example to the believers in word, in conduct, in love, in spirit, in faith, in purity.

- Paul

1 Corinthians 15:9
For I am the least of the apostles, who am not worthy to be called an apostle, because I persecuted the church of God.

• The disciples

Acts 4:13
Now when they saw the boldness of Peter and John, and perceived that they were uneducated and untrained men, they marveled. And they realized that they had been with Jesus.

Why don't you become the gatekeeper for your family?

3. **God uses people to do something different so they achieve different results.** Jacob was a tremendous example of someone with a limited past who overcame incredible odds. Jacob was stuck in a family system that was limited and dysfunctional. He and his mother conspired and deceived, to secure a father's blessing and inheritance. These two things really belonged to his brother Esau, as I mentioned earlier. The point I want to underscore one more time before we finish *The Transformed Family*, is this: Jacob set a chain-reaction of change in his family and society, by doing something different. Jacob decided to break the tradition of limited blessing, by blessing his two grandchildren. Not only does he bless them; he calls them *his*. He gave them the same inheritance as his other sons. Jacob broke with old traditions to set up a new order. Jacob's decision laid the foundation of the twelve tribe nation of Israel. How many blessings do you have to give to your descendants? Jacob gave birth to the prophetic movement.

Genesis 49:1
And Jacob called his sons and said, "Gather together, that I may tell you what shall befall you in the last days . . ."

Throughout the verses of Genesis 49, Jacob prophesied over his children and Joseph's two sons. That type of parental, prophetic gift had never been demonstrated before. Jacob developed a new understanding of blessing, while adding the component of prophetic images for each descendant. Jacob created a new tradition of rewarding and blessing, based on character, instead of tradition. His words to Joseph demonstrated the respect and blessings traditionally reserved to the firstborn only, but Jacob was creating a new path.

Genesis 49:22-24
"Joseph is a fruitful bough,
A fruitful bough by a well;
His branches run over the wall.
The archers have bitterly grieved him,
Shot at him and hated him.
But his bow remained in strength,
And the arms of his hands were made strong
By the hands of the Mighty God of Jacob
(From there is the Shepherd, the Stone of Israel) . . ."

Traditions are good when they give life, stability and reflect the spirit of God. However, God reserves the right to mess with all of our earthly traditions, in order to reward and bless, based on character and not position. Are there family habits or traditions that need to change in your home or church? Do your traditions open gates of the prophetic or close the door on the supernatural?

ARE YOU A GATEKEEPER?

God is looking for gatekeepers. He is looking for people that are qualified to open doors and close doors.

- He is looking for people that are committed to holiness and righteousness like Noah.

Genesis 6:9
This is the genealogy of Noah. Noah was a just man, perfect in his generations. Noah walked with God.

Genesis 7:1
Then the LORD said to Noah, "Come into the ark, you and all your household, because I have seen that you are righteous before Me in this generation."

• He is looking for people who have faith like Abraham.

Hebrews 11:8-10
By faith Abraham obeyed when he was called to go out to the place which he would receive as an inheritance. And he went out, not knowing where he was going. By faith he dwelt in the land of promise as in a foreign country, dwelling in tents with Isaac and Jacob, the heirs with him of the same promise; for he waited for the city which has foundations, whose builder and maker is God.

• He is looking for available people like Mary.

Luke 1:38
Then Mary said, "Behold the maidservant of the Lord! Let it be to me according to your word." And the angel departed from her.

• He is looking for people like you.

Isaiah 6:8
Also I heard the voice of the Lord, saying:
"Whom shall I send,
And who will go for Us?"
Then I said, "Here am I! Send me."

• He is looking for people with a contagious attitude.

Psalm 145:3-4
Great is the LORD, and greatly to be praised;
And His greatness is unsearchable.
One generation shall praise Your works to another,
And shall declare Your mighty acts.

As the pages of this book come to a close, I can't help but wonder what God will do through people like you and I. I am convinced that He wants to use families to transform cities. I am convinced that He always starts with one hungry soul who will overcome fear and intimidation, to usher in a new generation of change.

Joshua 1:6
"Be strong and of good courage, for to this people you shall divide as an inheritance the land which I swore to their fathers to give them."

Transformed families are healthy families. Healthy families are fruitful families. Fruitful families reflect God's heart for the world.

Genesis 1:22
And God blessed them, saying, "Be fruitful and multiply, and fill the waters in the seas, and let birds multiply on the earth."

Whether you are married, single, young, middle-aged or a senior, God is looking for gatekeepers. Will you answer His call?

GENERATIONAL IMPACT

John Manxwell's great book *Today Matters* highlights the generational impact of two men. As I read the accomplishments of the descendants of Jonathan Edwards and the struggles of the descendants of Dugdale, I was struck by this truth: *"Do not be deceived, God is not mocked; for whatever a man sows, that he will also reap"* (Galatians 6:7).

John Maxwell tells this amazing story of a man by the name of Richard L. Dugdale who was on the executive committee for the Prison Association of New York. He was assigned to inspect thirteen county jails in the state. While inspecting the jails, he discovered that six inmates were blood-related to him. He was very interested and decided to do a study on his family. He estimated that he had around 1,200 family members, but he could only trace 709 members. Dugdale discovered that his family had quite a pattern of criminal behavior: 180 were paupers, 140 were criminals, 60 were habitual thieves and 50 were common prostitutes.

Maxwell continues with a story about Jonathan Edwards: the theologian pastor and president of Princeton. A man named A.E. Winship studied 1,400 of Jonathan and Sarah (his wife) Edwards' descendants and discovered that there were 13 college presidents, 65 professors, 100 lawyers, 30 judges, 66 physicians and 80 holders of public office (which included 3 governors, 3 U.S. senators, 3 mayors of large cities, a controller of the U.S. Treasury and a U.S. Vice President).

Somehow, some way, these two men passed on dreams or nightmares, confidence or insecurity and resources or a spirit of poverty. If you could change the course of your family tree, would you? As you've read the previous pages, I'm sure that you understood how I feel. Yes, you can change the future of your family. Every seed you sow or gift you transfer will leave a generational impact. In fact, in most cases, there seems to be a multiplying effect on our future generations. They are several times more advanced (or worse) than we are now. Let's commit to God, that they will have a good seed and a firm foundation to build on.

This book was not written to exhaust the issue of impartation in the home, but to introduce you to it. I hope you will continue your study and apply these principles in your own home. I have included a resource guide at the end of this book, along with a list of recommended books that I believe will be a benefit to you.

Parents: Please do not underestimate how much you already impart into your children. You cannot help but impart to them, but what you do have control over is what you impart. Determine that you will begin to pour life, truth, love, vision and anointing into your children.

Even if you feel that you have nothing to offer, God can and will use you to impart something of value. Just humble yourself and ask Him. The woman with the single flask of oil demonstrates God's ability to increase what we pour out:

2 Kings 4:1-7

A certain woman of the wives of the sons of the prophets cried out to Elisha, saying, "Your servant my husband is dead, and you know that your servant feared the LORD. And the creditor is coming to take my two sons to be his slaves." So Elisha said to her, "What shall I do for you? Tell me, what do you have in the house?" And she said, "Your maidservant has nothing in the house but a jar of oil." Then he said, "Go, borrow vessels from everywhere, from all your neighbors—empty vessels; do not gather just a few. And when you have come in, you shall shut the door behind you and your sons; then pour it into all those vessels, and set aside the full ones." So she went from him and shut the door behind her and her sons, who brought the vessels to her; and she poured it out. Now it came to pass, when the vessels were full, that she said to her son, "Bring me another vessel." And he said to her, "There is not another vessel." So the oil ceased. Then she came and told the man of God. And he said, "Go, sell the oil and pay your debt; and you and your sons live on the rest."

We cannot control how our family will respond to the pouring that we commit to. As adults, we must accept that we are responsible for our thoughts, feelings and actions. To accept responsibility over these three will empower us to change for the good. If we change the way we think, it will change the way we feel and it will change the actions that we take. The prophet Elisha challenged the widow to reconsider what she had left in her home. At first, she said she had nothing, but all of the sudden, she remembered that she had kept a small flask of oil. Could this be the same oil used by her husband, the prophet? Was it cooking oil or oil for a small lamp? The text doesn't reveal that secret, but we know that it was significant to her, because she had sold everything else but this little flask of oil. The solution to all her problems was so simple, but hard. Gather empty jars and pour, pour, pour.

FILL EMPTY JARS

Isn't this a great prophetic sign for us, as parents? The world wants to take our children into slavery and God's solution is to keep pouring until all those seeds bear great fruit. I hope you can receive this word of faith. Take a moment and let God know how you feel, then tell Him: "Lord, I receive that word. I won't give up on my kids. I will keep pouring until you bring them into their destiny."

The little lad who gave up his sack lunch and watched, as the Lord used it to feed five-thousand people (John 6:8-11), learned the same truth. When we give with a sincere heart, God multiplies the good to feed the many. God has elected you as His vessel to pour truth into your children. You have been appointed and anointed to do so. Go ahead and begin today. Take some time and ask yourself the following questions: What do you pour the most of into your children? Have you reaped a harvest yet? If so, what has been the harvest?

LET THE RIVER OF CHANGE FLOW

Since transference, pouring and impartation are occurring in our homes daily, shouldn't we ask our heavenly Father to help us make it count for the good of our children? Let us determine to change the course of our family—and especially our children—through every choice we make, word we say and action we take. Jesus said:

John 7:38
"He who believes in Me, as the Scripture has said, out of his heart will flow rivers of living water."

Jesus was referring to the Holy Spirit. As we learn to let go of our lives and let ourselves flow along with the Holy Spirit, we will find the course of our own lives changing. We will have more to give and God will be able to use us more and more, to change the lives of others. To change the course of a family is a challenging, but extraordinarily worthwhile endeavor. It is like changing the course of a mighty river. Major construction must take place. It may take months or years to build the necessary dams, canals and fortification. Here are a few truths to remember, in redirecting the future of your family:

— ***It will take time to fully redirect it.*** Don't forget how long it took you to reach this point. You are the product of years of impartations, good and bad habits, decisions, circumstances and experiences.

— ***Each small step in the right direction will impact your family's future.*** We are not to despise *"the day of small things"* (Zechariah 4:10). Positive change always starts with one choice, by one person and, repeated over time, it yields a harvest.

— ***Repentance must be expressed and demonstrated.*** The Bible says, *"Humble yourselves in the sight of the Lord, and He will lift you up"* (James 4:10); and *"If we confess our sins, He is faithful and just to forgive us our sins and to cleanse us from all unrighteousness."* (1 John 1:9). Denise and I have humbled ourselves

before our children—as well as before the Lord—on more than
one occasion. We are imperfect people; it follows that we are
imperfect parents. A repentant spirit simply helps us to admit
that fact and helps keep everyone honest. It is also good for our
children to see us model humility, confession and repentance,
which are extremely important things to learn.

— *Our homes must be places where confession and forgiveness
are practiced and taught.* Simple sentences like, "Please forgive me" and "I forgive you" will set the stage for a home filled
with mercy, tenderness, grace and love. Where there is no forgiveness, bitterness, resentment, fear and depression will reign.
Jesus said, *"Forgive and you will be forgiven"* (Luke 6:37). The
Word also warns us: *"looking carefully lest anyone fall short of the
grace of God; lest any root of bitterness springing up cause trouble,
and by this many become defiled"* (Hebrews 12:15).

— *As you move forward in redirecting the course of your family,
you may find yourself facing generational curses.* The blood of
Jesus Christ and the power of the Holy Spirit can cancel the generational sins of our forefathers. As children of God, we have authority in Jesus' name, to break all curses and destroy strongholds. The Bible says, *"For the weapons of our warfare are not
carnal but mighty in God for pulling down strongholds, casting
down arguments and every high thing that exalts itself against the
knowledge of God, bringing every thought into captivity to the obedience of Christ"* (2 Corinthians 10:4-5). It also assures us that, *"in
all these things we are more than conquerors through Him who loved
us"* (Romans 8:37). Luke 10:19 also says, *"Behold, I give you the
authority to trample on serpents and scorpions, and over all the power
of the enemy, and nothing shall by any means hurt you."*

— *The promises of God are for you and your family. Claim these promises for your home.* Stand on His Word. Let your faith reach out to God for the salvation of your family. The jailer of Paul and Silas was told, *"Believe on the Lord Jesus and you will be saved; you and your household"* (Acts 16:31).

PRAY FOR THE RIVER OF GOD

In the book of Ezekiel, the prophet saw a river coming from the temple:

Ezekiel 47:1-2

Then he brought me back to the door of the temple; and there was water, flowing from under the threshold of the temple toward the east, for the front of the temple faced east; the water was flowing from under the right side of the temple, south of the altar. He brought me out by way of the north gate, and led me around on the outside to the outer gateway that faces east; and there was water, running out on the right side.

This river is symbolic of more than one thing, but one of them is most likely a prophecy of the work of the Holy Spirit under the New Covenant, when the body of each believer would become the temple of the Holy Spirit. Revelation 22:1 says, *"And he showed me a pure river of water of life, clear as crystal, proceeding from the throne of God and of the Lamb."* The river was revealed and it covers the throne of heaven. Wow. Isn't that incredible? The river was also declared to be healing for the nations (Revelation 22:2). Do you know that God wants to live inside of you and flow out from your life, like it did in Ezekiel's vision? I Corinthians asks us this question:

1 Corinthians 6:19
Or do you not know that your body is the temple of the Holy Spirit who is in you, whom you have from God, and you are not your own?

The river of God must flow through you, to your family, as it did in Ezekiel. When it does, your family will be changed forever. Why shouldn't our entire household be saved, healed, delivered and used by God? We can become like Abraham—who was the pivotal portal of blessing for his family—or like Rahab. She saw the hand of God and responded in faith. Her faith saved her family and changed many generations. There is no limit to what God can do through prayer and fasting. God can use you to initiate a move that will bless your family for generations to come.

LISTEN TO GOD

As I mentioned earlier, about a year ago my son was diagnosed with a life-threatening disease. It was during this time that God spoke to me powerfully in service one day. As most of you probably know, I don't hear voices; however, I do receive thoughts that lead me and guide me. Don't forget that He speaks with a still, small voice (1Kings 19:12). So, when God spoke to me during that service, it was as clear as day. The question entered my mind: "Paul, do you really want to see your son healed?" I answered, "Yes." Again, a question came to me: "Paul, do you want to build prayer mountain?" I said, "Yes." He then said, "Then give me your pay checks for the rest of the year." Wow! I was shocked, but I knew that it was God. I committed to this huge sacrifice, as long as my wife would agree, which she did.

So, we embarked on a journey of faith that proved to be incredible. Not only did my son get healed, he was called to be in full-time ministry and our bank account ended this year higher than ever before. God is great! God wants to speak to you and through you. He wants to lead you and your family. It is a great journey!

If you have given your life to Jesus Christ, you are the temple of His Holy Spirit. Allow Him to flow through you in a new way. He will pour life into your family, home and children. If you have never surrendered your life to Jesus Christ, please take a moment to pray this prayer:

"Dear Jesus, I need you. Please come into my heart, my life and my family. Forgive me for all my failures and sins. Make me new and fill me with Your Holy Spirit, so that my children and I will have a future and a hope. Amen."

If you prayed this prayer, please contact me through our website at: www.iclv.com. There is a list of helpful material for you and your family, available through email at the same web site. The truths of the Bible will unleash a whole new world to you and your family.

You may also contact us by calling (702) 242-2273 or by sending mail to:

International Church of Las Vegas
8100 Westcliff Drive
Las Vegas, NV 89145

We want to invite you to tune into our online TV network for tons of programming, music, encouragement, inspiration and even live services at: www.SpiritFlowTV.com.

RESOURCE GUIDE

Gary Chapman, *The Five Love Languages: How to Express Heartfelt Commitment to Your Mate* (Chicago, IL : Northfield Publishing, 1992)

Richard D. Dobbins, *Invisible Imprint* (Akron, OH : Totally Alive Publications, 2002)

James C. Dobson, *Dare to Discipline* (Wheaton, IL : Tyndale House Publishers, 1970, 1992)

Hal Donaldson & Kenneth M. Dobson, *Parenting: Successful Church Leaders Share Biblical Principles for Raising Kids in the Nineties* (Sacramento, CA : Onward Books, Inc., 1993)

Paul M. Goulet, *The Breakthrough Series* (Las Vegas, NV : ICLV, 1999)

Paul M. Goulet, *The Power of Impartation: Seven Keys to Unlock the Power of God in Your Life* (Las Vegas, NV : ICLV, 2002)

Paul M. Goulet, *Crossing Your Next Threshold: Seven Steps to Help You Enter into Your Promised Land*, Las Vegas, NV : ICLV, 2006)

Paul M. Goulet, *The 5 Powers of God* (Nashville, TN : Thomas Nelson, 2007)

Paul M. Goulet, *The Vision Bible* (Las Vegas, NV : ICLV, 2007, in association with Thomas Nelson)

Dr. Tim Elmore, *Nurturing the Leader Within Your Child* (Nashville, TN : Thomas Nelson, 2001)

Dr. Josh McDowell, *Evidence that Demands a Verdict* (Campus Crusade for Christ, 1972)

Robert S. McGee, *The Search for Significance* (Dallas, TX : W Publishing Group, 1998)

John Maxwell, *The 360 Degree Leader* (Nashville, TN : Thomas Nelson, 2006)

OTHER BOOKS BY PAUL GOULET

The 5 Powers of God

In this book, Pastor Paul Goulet introduces and describe the five powers of God. Goulet helps you move toward a better understanding of the Holy Spirit, by bringing you to an understanding of His powers. As you unlock the mysterious connection between the forms of God's power, you will be able to extend it beyond the walls of your local church, into the realm of daily life.

Vision Bible

In this new *Vision Bible* you will find an introduction by Paul Goulet, that reveals vision as a theme, throughout the whole Bible. The Bible is not only about the people of God who had vision for their lives; it is also about God's vision for all of humanity. Discover God's vision for your life, with the new *Vision Bible*.

Crossing Your Next Threshold

God has designated threshold moments in your life. A threshold is a moment of transition, in which a decision can change your future. In *Crossing Your Next Threshold* you will discover seven key revelations that will help you see and seize these opportunities.

Power of Impartation

Jesus prophesied that the believers in Jerusalem would receive power after the Holy Spirit came upon them. Do you have this type of power in your life? Learn how impartation can empower you to heal, preach, win souls and walk in a new anointing.

30 Day Journey to Spiritual Health

30 Day Journey to Spiritual Health is a tool that will revolutionize your spiritual walk and help you go deeper with God than ever before. Combining their shared decades of experience in pastoral ministry and counseling, **Pastors Paul and Denise Goulet** have designed a 30 day plan to coach & educate you on key Biblical truths while helping you gain a clear concept of God the Father and His love for you.

Visit us Online at www.iclv.com

Don't forget that there are many other resources that can help you continue on in this journey. Visit www.spiritflow.net to access a steady stream of free resources and our bookstore. Our online church could also be a blessing to you and your friends looking for a dynamic church.